BARBADOS DIVE GUIDE

First published in 2005 in Barbados by Miller Publishing Company
This second edition published in 2015 in the UK by Scuba Channels Ltd

ScubaChannels

Maidenhead, Berkshire, UK
W: www.scubachannels.com
E: admin@scubachannels.com

Copyright © Lucy Agace 2015

All text by Lucy Agace • All rights reserved
All photographs by Lucy Agace unless otherwise stated

Marketed and distributed by Scuba Channels Ltd

Designed by Patricia Hopkins

All rights reserved. No part of this publication may be reproduced, stored in a retrieval system, or transmitted, in any form or by any means, electronic, mechanical, photocopying, recording or otherwise, without the prior written permission of the copyright owners and publishers.

ISBN: 978-0-9933912-0-0

Printed in China

TABLE OF CONTENTS

- 4 AUTHOR
- 6 BARBADOS OVERVIEW
- 8 WHAT'S NEW
- 10 CLIMATE/CONDITIONS
- 11 ESSENTIAL INFORMATION
- 12 RECREATION
- 16 BARBADOS DIVING
- 25 HYPERBARIC CHAMBER
- 28 BARBADOS DIVE CENTRES
- 45 DIVE SITE MAP
- 46 SHARKS HOLE
- 49 MAYCOCKS
- 50 CEMENT PLANT PIER
- 55 BRIGHT LEDGE
- 56 PAMIR
- 61 GREAT LEDGE
- 63 THE FARM
- 65 SPAWNEE
- 67 WHITEGATES
- 69 TROPICANA
- 70 LONESTAR
- 71 MERLIN BAY
- 73 CHURCH POINT
- 75 DOTTINS REEF
- 77 SANDY LANE
- 79 BOMBAS REEF
- 80 FISHERMANS
- 83 CRYSTAL COVE
- 85 VICTOR'S REEF
- 86 SS STAVRONIKITA
- 93 BELL BUOY
- 94 CLARKES BANK
- 96 CARLISLE BAY WRECKS
- 101 OLD FORT
- 103 CASTLE BANK
- 104 FRIARS CRAIG & RUM BARREL & ASTA REEF
- 109 CARLEYNE
- 111 PIECES OF EIGHT
- 113 CARIBEE
- 115 THE BOOT
- 117 THE MUFF
- 119 ST LAWRENCE REEF
- 121 CLOSE ENCOUNTERS/ DOVER
- 123 HIGHWIRE
- 125 MOUNT CHARLIE
- 127 THE FINGER
- 129 GRAEME HALL SHALLOWS
- 131 THE STUDY
- 133 RAGGED POINT
- 139 BARBADOS UNDERWATER PHOTOGRAPHY ACADEMY
- 140 SEAHORSES
- 142 INDEX

ACKNOWLEDGEMENTS

I would like to express my appreciation to Henrietta Passos, whose energy and determination knows no bounds and her love of underwater photography and appreciation for marine life is clearly measured by her wonderful photographs in this book.
Thank you to Gay Taaffe, Niki Farmer and Sam Greening for their proof reading and general angelic support.
Thank you to the staff at all the dive centres and to all the friends and companies who have supported this edition.

Lucy Agace's Story

Publishing this 2nd edition Barbados dive guide has been a great pleasure, especially diving new sites and discovering amazing new critters. Perhaps the real beauty of the underwater world is the fact that it is ever changing, we never know what we are going to see or find on a dive. For me, every dive is an adventure armed with my camera a photo or video opportunity. What could be better?

Being a diver for over thirty years, and having visited all of the major oceans as well as eighty percent of the Caribbean islands, I believe I am well placed to say that the quality of diving in Barbados rivals any other found in the Lesser Antilles. I still get excited about diving in Barbados, even though I have dived all over the world, such is the richness and variety of marine life here.

Since the arrival of good quality compact digital cameras and affordable housings almost every diver now has a camera. Underwater photography and videography have become both a reason to dive and something else to do whilst diving. Are you diving to photograph or photographing dives?

This is one of the reasons I built a new website **www.scubachannels.com** to provide a copyright free platform for people to post their work, free of charge, so why not become a member too? For information see back cover.

My love of the world beneath the waves began in the 1970's watching the ground breaking underwater documentaries of Jacques Cousteau. Cousteau, inspired the world and left me with no doubt as to where I wanted to go. I learnt to dive in the mid 80's in Jamaica, my first dive filled me with awe and wonder. My husband and I then spent the next three years diving the Caribbean and the Red Sea. During this time I attempted to master the art of underwater photography, which had become my passion and the focus of my diving.

Then in 1987 we set off on a voyage around the world that would take six years, a once in a lifetime trip. We dived some of the most inaccessible islands, the largest atolls and survived cyclones and sharks. We dived famous dive destinations like: Truk, Palau, Tonga, Thailand, the Maldives and Galapagos Islands, as well as little known areas like: the Tuamotus, Cocos, Chagos, Solomons and many islands in Indonesia. We were our own guides and explored little known areas in the middle of no-where, using just our knowledge and nautical maps for guidance.

Cocos Island, a relatively unknown destination at the time is now considered a top dive spot in the world and the best place to see schooling hammerhead sharks. I was so amazed by the experience of the whole island I decided to write a book about it: 'Dive Guide to Cocos Island' is now only available on ebay or here at www.scubachannels.com/dive-books.

Lastly, we travelled up the entire length of the Red Sea in one fabulous seven-week trip, the highlight of which was diving off Port Sudan with dolphins. What a privilege this trip was, because I'm not even sure this kind of journey would be possible in the world today.

A few years ago I decided to change my camera from a DSLR system to a compact digital one and now use a Lumix LX5 and an Olympus XZ-2 with two INON D2000 strobes. I have found both systems to be very portable and user friendly. I am an INON Level 1 instructor and formed the (BUPA) Barbados Underwater Photography Academy in 2014. I spend over half the year on the island and can provide both private and group tuition. For more details please visit -http://scubachannels.ccm/bupa and page 139 of this guide book.

I am often asked which are my favourite Barbados dive sites. It's very hard to choose but I recommend you dive west and south coast sites. My favourites are: Cement Plant Pier (wide angle and critters), the Stavronikita wreck (wide angle with fish and corals), Carlisle Bay Marine Park wrecks, marine life variety) and Bell Buoy (hard corals).

The intention of this dive guide is to ensure that scuba divers get the very best out of their diving experiences whilst here. You will be fore-armed with the knowledge you need to make informed decisions and it also serves as a handy tourist guide to the many other activities.

I hope you enjoy this book and most importantly I hope you visit Barbados and have many wonderful diving experiences.

My very best wishes,

Lucy Agace

BARBADOS

An island of immense charm, natural beauty and character, Barbados has everything to offer holiday makers from all over the world and from all walks of life. Picture the warm sparkle of the Caribbean Sea; 365 days of sunshine each year and beautiful sandy beaches which can either offer every conceivable amusement, or can be tranquil and deserted. Barbados has it all.

Barbados lies in the Lesser Antilles, a chain of islands in the eastern Caribbean which is divided into two groups - the northerly Leeward islands, and the southerly Windward islands. Barbados is located just east of the Windward island chain, about 100 miles east of St. Vincent.

The capital of Barbados is Bridgetown, a busy hub of activity where sports fishing boats and charter sailing vessels nestle alongside waterfront restaurants, and duty free shops. Accommodation ranges from some of the most luxurious hotels and villas in the Caribbean to competitively priced holiday packages and all-inclusive resorts. Perhaps it is a combination of these factors which has given Barbados the prestigious honour of being the island most visitors return to - over and over again - in the Caribbean.

Barbadians, or 'Bajans' as they affectionately call themselves, are warm and relaxed people who relate well with the constant flow of multicultural and cosmopolitan visitors. The island enjoys strong links with Britain, Canada, the United States, and many parts of Europe, and the influence of these countries can easily be seen in many aspects of the island's cultural development.

The rhythm of the sea is at the heart of Barbados, and it plays out in the island's unique brand of Calypso music, served with just the right amount of Barbados rum. Part of the magic of the island is its two distinctly different coasts - the east and the west. The cut-glass western shoreline tantalizes the eye as the crystal-clear ocean gently rolls on to white sandy beaches, canopied by coconut-laden palm trees. This side of the island is calm and protected, and is gently caressed by the Caribbean Sea.

An evening sail on Reeds Bay

View of the east coast. By Lucy Agace

The east coast, however, is quite the opposite, for here the wind rules the waves and creates a pounding surf and a rugged, free-spirited atmosphere which is unequalled anywhere. The Atlantic Ocean dominates the lifestyle of this coast - there are only a few hotels, bars and restaurants, and life in general is slower-paced. The near empty beaches stretch for miles, and a long walk allows the mind and body to soak-up all 4 elements. There is a wave of spirituality that is palpable. Indeed, these two cultures of east coast and west coast complement each other perfectly, giving the island's natural structure both balance and variety.

A little bit of History - It was not until the mid 17th century that Barbados was colonised by the English over a period of many years, 1625 - 1644. During this time, much of the land in Barbados was cleared for the creation of cotton, tobacco and sugar cane plantations which were worked by indentured workers and African slaves. Slavery was abolished in 1834 but almost the entire labouring class continued to live and work on the plantations and factories. Bridgetown has a number of historical sites which include the Garrison, museums and galleries. Such is their significance, in 2011 Bridgetown was included in the UNESCO list of World Heritage Sites.

Although not as mountainous as other Caribbean islands, the rolling hills of Barbados provides the perfect environment for sugar cane crops to flourish. Today sugar remains the island's largest export and its production fuels two economies - the cane sugar is refined into both table sugar as well as into rum, both integral parts of life in Barbados and both equally successful products. Barbados remained a British colony until 1961 when internal autonomy was granted and full independence followed in 1966.

2016 is the '50th Anniversary Year Of Independence' for Barbados and will be marked by many island-wide celebrations.

HAZELL'S WATER WORLD
BAY STREET, BRIDGETOWN

P: +1 (246) 426 4043
E: contact@hazellswaterworld.com
W: www.diversupplybarbados.com

Open hours: Tues to Sat 10am - 5pm
Closed for lunch 12.30-1.30pm

Hazell's Water World (Divers Supply Barbados) is the only diving equipment stockist on the island.

John Hazell is a Padi instructor who has been diving since the 1970's and has a wealth of local diving knowledge and experience in the industry.

John Hazell believes customers should be able to see, feel and try on equipment before they buy it. Hazell's offers great advice and tailor-made recommendations, because to him 'no one diver is the same' and he makes every effort to ensure customer satisfaction.

The only authorised dealer on the island, Hazell's stocks a good selection of Tusa, Cressi and Mares diving and snorkelling equipment (including children's sizes). They also sell rash guards, wetsuits, T-shirts, books, fish ID cards, reef shoes, divers boots, pole spears for catching Lionfish and many small useful items.

Hazell's stocks a range of diving accessories such as: dive lights, dive flags, surface buoys, SMB's reels, swim googles, mask straps, dive slates, knives, lanyards, orthodontic mouth pieces, computer batteries, dive bags and cameras. They stock an excellent selection of the brand HeadWare which provides sun protection on land and keeps hair under control whilst diving.

There are manufacturer warranties on all in-store sales and a discount on servicing of equipment originally purchased from Hazell's. They also offer a certified gear and repair service.

PROMOTIONS:
Visitors
TAX-FREE SHOPPING is available to visitors. You must show your passport and airline ticket, and cruise ship passengers must show their cruise ship ID.
Residents.
Present this book and receive **10% DISCOUNT** on all retail purchases.

RESTRICTIONS: Valid for cash sales only. Does not apply to products on sale or items already discounted.

What's new in Edition II - Through the continued work of the Coastal Zone Management Unit the Barbados government is taking steps to establish a marine park fee for divers, payable once yearly. This is long over due and maybe partly implemented by 2016.

The invasive Lionfish species arrived here about 4 years ago, roughly 10 years behind the first sightings of these fish in the Bahamas. They are ferocious predators and reproduce at alarming rates - every 4 days! A single female can spawn over 2 million eggs per year and they can eat up to 30 times their stomach volume. I am pleased to say they are hunted daily by local fisherman and divers.

Lionfish fillet is available in fish markets and some restaurants, it is delicious! Beware when diving, Lionfish have venomous spines on their back that can deliver an extremely painful sting if touched. If stung, immerse the injured area in hot water and seek medical attention.

We have 6 new fabulous dive sites, two of which are on the east coast, The Study and Ragged Point. In the north - Sharks Hole and Cement Plant Pier have been added and down the west coast Bell Buoy. In addition the south has Carlsyne.

There is a Lionfish Derby held once a year and anyone is welcome. Please see link below for details.

For more details please visit:
www.barbadoslionfishderby.com

Climate - Conditions - Barbados is unique among the Caribbean islands in many ways, and its geological origin also sets it apart. Unlike most of the windward island chain, the birth of Barbados was not due to a violent volcanic movement. Instead, it came about as a result of tectonic plate uplifts and a gradual elevation of raised oceanic deposits and coral reef formation. Today dozens of underground streams have carved their way through the island's limestone bedrock and have created a network of caves. The most spectacular of these can be seen at Harrison's Cave which is located in the parish of St. Thomas. Here there are underground pools, tumbling waterfalls, and fabulous stalagmite and stalactite formations.

Barbados is 21 miles long and 14 miles wide and lies 13° north of the equator. Temperatures can vary from 22°C at night to 32°C during the day. Divers can enjoy warm water temperatures throughout the year, varying from 25°C in the 'winter' months Dec - April to 29°C in the summer months July - Sept. Divers can wear anything from skin suits to 4mm full wetsuits depending on how much they feel the cold or dive for an hour or more.

Though the Trade Winds offer year-round relief from the hot sun, the Easter (or kite flying) months of March and April are often windy. The wet season is from June to October, when tropical storms can affect the entire Caribbean and eastern United States at this time. I have, in fact, experienced Barbadian summers with only two days of rain, light breezes and therefore wonderful diving during the summer months. So, don't be put off by the rainy season if this is your preferred time of travel. The dry season is from Jan - June.

In the summer months the humidity increases and the seas can often be at their calmest and most tranquil.

The setting sun on the west coast.
By Lucy Agace

Sea temperatures at this time can reach 29°C and underwater visibility can be excellent. But this does not mean good visibility is restricted to these months.

All of the beaches on Barbados are public and easily accessible. The famous Crane Beach on the southeast coast is touted for its soft, pink sand - some of the finest to be found in the Caribbean. There are also dozens of beautiful beaches running along the west and south coasts of the island. And over on the eastern shore there is the East Coast Beach which runs almost uninterrupted for 5 miles, from Barclays Park southward to Bath.

The lush tropical vegetation flourishes on the higher areas and ridges of the island and supports a variety of garden centres filled with tropical flowers. Probably the most extraordinary example of this is Hunte's Gardens, St Joseph; tranquility and splendour all in one.

Hunte's Garden

ESSENTIAL INFORMATION:

MONEY:
Both US$ and Bds$ are accepted. The B$ is tied to the USD at a rate of USD1 = Bds$1.98

CARS:
Drive on the left, like the UK.

DRESS CODE:
No nudity on beaches, keep swimwear on.
Camouflage is prohibited

ELECTRICITY:
110/230V 50Hz

TAX:
17.5%

TIPPING:
10 - 15%

WATER:
Tap water is safe to drink

RECREATION

Myles hits a drive at Royal Westmoreland golf club.

Barbados is more than just another luxurious island paradise. Besides diving, there is a wide range of activities which include golf, sailing regattas, paddle boarding, polo, tennis, horse racing, cycling, surfing, cricket, off-road rallying, big game fishing, kayaking, hiking, visits to wildlife reserves, and of course, shopping.

Top quality golf is available at the Barbados Golf Club, Apes Hill, Sandy Lane, and Royal Westmoreland. The Barbados Golf Club welcomes visitors and you can hire equipment. The recently renovated Sandy Lane offers two 18-hole golf courses, and the Sandy Lane Hotel itself - with its fine dining, exclusive villas, and fabulous spa, is often classed as the Caribbean's finest resort. The Royal Westmoreland golf course opened in 1994 and because it's set in an elevated position, this course has breath-taking views of the western coast. Visitors are also welcome to play the 9-hole public course at the The Rockley Golf Club in Christ Church. This course is reasonably well kept and rents equipment.

There are also strong polo and horse racing programs throughout the year, highlighted by the Sandy Lane Gold Cup held at the Garrison Savannah Race Track each year in early March. Polo matches are played in May at Lion Castle, Apes Hill and Holders, all friendly occasions and great fun.

Cricket, however, is the undisputed national sport and is played by people of all ages all over the island. International test cricket and one day series games are usually played from March to June, at the Kensington Oval, Bridgetown.

20/20 cricket at the Kensington Oval, Bridgetown.

Snorkelling - If you are visiting the island for a short time it is recommended to use one of the many safari boats, found on any beach, to aid you. These boats offer 2-3 hour excursions to the various marine parks or to snorkel with turtles. Safari boat operators use fish and bread to attract the turtles and it has now become a regular food source for the turtles. I would normally be against such unnatural feeding rituals but I have seen many visitors - previously afraid of the water and what lives in it - overcome their fear and get in the water to see the turtles close-up, leaving them with 'life changing" experiences.

The west coast has two designated snorkelling areas, both within the Folkestone Marine Park. One is situated in a large buoyed-off area in Holetown and you can swim out from the beach here. Sadly the reef is not very vibrant, although there are many signs of renewed coral growth, and marine life is present but sparse. The second park is situated a short distance from the beach in Holetown and most people get there by using the aforementioned safari boats which can be found along any beach. This second park has a purposely-sunk barge, which has attracted a wealth of marine life. The whole area is teaming with fish such as chubs (Locals call them Robins), sergeant

A hawksbill turtle comes up for air. By Lucy Agace

majors, damselfish, chromis and wrasse. At lower levels in the wreck it is possible to see eels, squirrelfish and snapper and, on the surrounding reef, parrotfish, trumpetfish, butterfly fish, surgeonfish, and smooth trunkfish passing by on their daily quest for food.

For the intrepid snorkeler a daring swim over shallow rocky areas in calm seas can be very rewarding, this is particularly good for finding small creatures such as lettuce slugs, starfish, tiny pencil stars and sea urchins.

The main snorkelling area in the south coast is the Carlisle Bay Marine Park. This protected park is much larger than the west coast parks and houses six wrecks. There is a dive site page for this area. It is easily accessed from the beach near the bandstand on the coast road.
But of course you can snorkel off the beach almost anywhere and just have a look and see what's there!

ATLANTIS SUBMARINES BARBADOS (INC)

The Shallow Draught, Bridgetown
Reservations: (246) 436 8929   8 a.m to 9 p.m
W: barbados.atlantissubmarines.com
E: bdsres@atlantissubmarines.com

 tripadvisor

BOOK ONLINE & SAVE

Atlantis Submarines have been operating a top quality service in Barbados since 1986 and received many awards for the following: hospitality, green globe, business excellence, sustainable tourism, top global experience and environmental awareness.

The 65 foot submarine takes 48 passengers down to depths varying between 50-150 feet in safe, dry luxury! Take a fully narrated day dive across beautiful reefs teaming with life, a wonderful experience for all ages (Min height 3 feet), a great family activity.

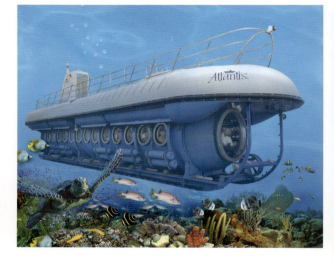

You can enhance your experience with a tour upgrade to VIP. Atlantis Submarines will accommodate a minimum of two VIP guests on each tour or a maximum of eight VIP guests in a group so the individual attention is guaranteed. Among other things you will get priority seating at the front of the submarine next to the pilot, special cocktail and hors d'oeuvres served on your return.

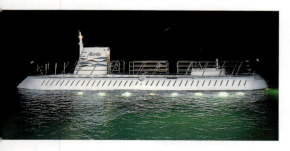

The night dives which were introduced in 2011 present a very different view of the coral reef. The use of high powered spot lights on the submarine highlight and enhance the natural colours of the reef making it overwhelmingly vibrant. Barbados is one of only two places in the world where this can be experienced, so take advantage whilst you are here!

Private and Five Star Champagne charters and events are available by special request only, they are not a regular event. Available for groups of 10 - 22 persons let the friendly helpful crew make sure you have an unforgettable experience. Email your requests directly and take a trip of a lifetime.

You travel in air conditioned comfort and during the voyage, over the reefs the pilot will take you to see a ship wreck which lies at around 130 feet. Feel free to take photos along the way.

Atlantis Submarines headquarters are based in Bridgetown's commercial port in the shallow draught area which is near the cruise ship terminal. From here a comfortable motored catamaran takes you out to the submarine which is just outside the port entrance. You are safely supervised onto the submarine by the staff and become fully submerged on a ride that lasts about 40 minutes.

For those that can't dive this represents a fabulous opportunity to see for yourself marine life living in its natural habitat, reefs covered in beautiful corals, brightly coloured fish, turtles and rays.

Atlantis Submarines will happily plan your special event for you. It is the perfect place to propose, share a special moment or even get married.

ENDORSEMENT:

When we went into the submarine, you are helped onboard by the staff, who are at all times concerned with your safety. The submarine is very light, air conditioned and doesn't feel claustrophobic in the slightest, each person has a seat and a large window. We had a staff member narrating what we saw. It was amazing to see the fish in their natural habitat.

BARBADOS DIVING OVERVIEW

With over 39 dive sites to chose from Barbados has something for every diver; wether its wrecks, marine life or just enjoying the underwater world, Barbados has it all. Not only are there flourishing, brightly coloured reefs covered in a variety of hard and soft corals, but there is a superb selection of wrecks - old and new, large and small. They are all complemented by a profusion of beautiful Caribbean reef and pelagic fish.

You can clearly see the upside down U shape of the reef, as divers descend onto Bright Ledge.

Barbados is blessed with two distinct barrier reefs and fringing reefs, which are all ideal for diving. One barrier reef runs parallel to the west coast and the other runs along the south coast shoreline. Both barrier reefs are separated from the shore by deep 'lagoons' and the fringing reefs lie alongside the shore in both of these areas. The barrier reefs take the brunt of any passing storms but the inner fringing reefs are still susceptible to surges and swells depending on the seasons and moon cycles. In general, both the west and south reefs have similar characteristics, but with some exceptions.

The **barrier reef sites** are shaped like an upside down 'U' where the top is between 50 - 80 feet across and tends to vary from a starting depth of 50 - 70 feet. Some of the reefs slope down to depths greater than 200 feet, too deep for recreational diving. Divers can travel at their own pace along the length of the reef and although there is plenty to see, it is also advisable to keep one eye on the open ocean side in case something interesting comes by, like an eagle ray, tarpon or a whaleshark.

The inner sites on the fringing reefs tend to be shallow, flatter and sandy but are often broken up by large 'islands' of branching or finger coral communities. Soft coral growth such as sea plumes and sea whips

A typical Barbados reef scene, taken on Maycocks reef. All photographs taken by Lucy Agace unless otherwise stated.

appear regularly but the corals have not grown densely, leaving lots of sandy spaces on the reef. However, there is no shortage of marine life, everything from atlantic squid, frogfish, garden eels and crabs to eagle rays, turtles and tiny flamingo tongue snails are found. These are the calmer, more protected sites and are usually excellent for close-up or macro photography and, of course, for student or novice divers.

Spring, a season beginning in March or April and associated with breeding in the animal kingdom, holds true here. In these months there are more juvenile fish on the reefs in Barbados and, I believe, more fish in general.

They come out of hiding to mate and subsequently we can often see more of everything, especially on the shallow fringing reefs. As with many heavily populated islands, there is some damage to corals on the fringing reefs due to such things as pollution, anchors and spear fishing. However, none of these are a major problem in themselves.

Schools of common reef fish like snappers, yellow goatfish, blue tang, sennet, chromis and creole wrasse are seen throughout the reefs and around the wrecks. Barbados is also home to many large pelagic fish such as, various species of jacks, tarpon, rainbow runner and mackerels.

Sting rays, eagle rays and many eels are common residents, plus the occasional sightings of manta rays, sharks (only on the north and east coasts) and whale sharks! Migrating humpback whales pass by on their way north between January - March, they can be seen jumping in the water all around the island. Their return journey usually takes place between September - October.

Pink encrusting sponge and encrusting fire coral have taken over this sea fan.

If a reef has a multitude of healthy corals it usually follows that the fish life is equally rich. One could say its a symbiotic relationship, they both need each other to co-exist in their ecological roles. If one declines its sure to follow that the other one will decline too. Luckily, the reverse is also true.

It is well documented that Caribbean reefs have suffered, over the last decade, from the combined impact of El Nino weather effects and over fishing; as has the rest of the world.

However, in general the majority of hard corals on Barbados reefs survived and coral re-generation is very much in evidence. Where corals die other corals take over and the balance of nature returns.

Present year-round, and particularly popular with everyone, are turtles. Three types of turtle visit the island - the hawksbill, green and leatherback. Only the leatherback and hawksbill actually make nests and lay eggs on Barbados. The green turtle is a visitor feeding on sea grasses and algae on the south and east coast. A small number of leatherbacks nest on the east coast beaches (March 1st – July 31st) but they are not seen on the reefs.

Green or Hawksbill turtles are common on most dive sites and are often seen around the many wrecks. If you visit Barbados between June to September, you could see Hawksbill turtles nesting on beaches on the west and south coasts.

The eggs take between 55-75 days to incubate so hatching season is mid July to mid October.

A turtle lays eggs on Hastings beach at night.

The **BARBADOS SEA TURTLE PROJECT (BSTP)** operates a 24 hour call line to report any nesting or hatching activity.

Call (246) 230-0142
or visit their website:
www.barbadosseaturtles.org
to find out when the next hatchling release is (only in season).

Hawksbill turtles are critically endangered due to over exploitation. In 1987 Prof. Julia Horrocks, of the University of the West Indies, founded the BSTP to restore local turtle populations, through monitoring programmes, implementation of training, education and public awareness tools and so much more. They run a highly rewarding volunteer program every year, please visit their website for more information.

Vitor Passos with his son Alexander and daughter Maya. By Henrietta Passos

July - August, so this is the best time to dive. All dives leave from Consett Bay from the fish market pier. It's a rough ride and seasick pills are advisable.

Generally, the underwater seascape is of giant rock boulders and bedrock where a few corals have managed to take hold. Sightings of sharks, rays, schooling fish and abstract shapes make diving here attractive.

Baby turtles in a bucket ready to be released into the sea.

The pounding waves and rough seas that hit the **East coast** make diving here very hard to plan and execute. However, the sea is usually much calmer in the summer months from

The southern reefs of Barbados are more susceptible to currents of varying strengths that prevail throughout the year. These currents bring the food necessary to sustain the forests of sea fans, sea plumes and gorgonias that populate the outer reefs. These reefs are covered in a wealth of sponges in all shapes and sizes, and you are more likely to see eagle rays here. Reefs start quite deep at 70 feet and some outer dive sites have quite steep sides, most notably the two furthest ones. They lie quite far off shore so the visibility is less likely to be effected by any run off caused by heavy rainfall.

I could almost describe Barbados as the Lembeh (Lembeh Straits famous for critters and muck diving) of the Caribbean, there are so many different types of **critters** here. There are rare species such as; seahorses, frogfish, jawfish, sailfin blennies, pipefish, batfish and mantis shrimps. Many of these can be found on one dive site - the Cement Plant Pier, but also on other dive sites.

Pike Blenny

Sailfin Blenny

Green Frogfish

Banded Jawfish

Longnose Seahorse

At night basket starfish open up and feed.

exceptional diversity of the sponges, especially further north, that sets the west apart from the southern reefs. The sponge growth is greater here and, in some cases, startling in its diversity and colour intensity; orange, purple, green and yellow.

The majority of the basket star population inhabit the southern reefs and spend most of the day bundled up in the arms of sea plumes. There are also many crinoids to be found here. Crinoids are members of the echinoderm family and not as common in the Caribbean as they are in the Pacific and Indian Oceans.

An amazing huge specimen of lavender sponge.

Hawksbill turtle eating Benthic sponge

While turtles are common on many dive sites on both coasts, a dive site in the south called the 'Boot' is where you are more likely to see the most turtles in one place, perhaps because generous amounts of their food - benthic sponge, is found there.

An undulating barrier reef runs up the entire length of the **west coast** from Victors' Reef up to Bright Ledge, almost without interruption. What really stands out on these west coast reefs is the amount of hard corals and colourful sponges. It is the

The reefs around Speightstown are famous for the beautiful falling arms of the brown octopus sponge, and some barrel sponges have grown so big they are the size of a bath!

The further north you travel along the reefs you will notice good quantities of many hard corals - star, plate, brain - interspersed with sea fans, and gorgonians. But one of the best reefs to see the healthiest collection of hard corals is the dive Bell Buoy.

Please be careful whilst diving here, so as not to break or touch any corals, we would like to keep them healthy.

Mid water schooling fish such as; creole wrasse, boga and chromis act as filter feeders above the reefs and in doing this, play an important ecological role. These schools are present on all the dive sites up the west and south coasts and bring colour and action to dives, plus for the photographer a useful shape changing, moving subject. Atlantic spade fish, jacks, rainbow runners and cero - a large species of mackerel - are also regularly seen flashing across reefs from the direction of the open ocean.

Barbados undoubtedly has the best collection of wrecks in the Caribbean. Standing above all others, quite literally, is the SS Stavronikita, a 365 foot long freighter which was sunk on purpose in 1978. This impressive wreck is now covered in beautiful corals, sponges and fish life and is the most often re-dived site in Barbados.

The picturesque Carlisle Bay lies a short walk from Bridgetown and

Robert leaps over the sun! By Lucy Agace

is the resting place of a group of wrecks located in the Carlisle Bay Marine Park. The park contains six wrecks of varying age and size and they are easily accessible to both snorkelers and scuba divers from the beach. This is a very popular dive site and many of the sailing cruise boats come here too.

There are two other wrecks that are in fact sister ships, the Pamir, located on the west coast, and the Friar's Craig on the south coast. They were both deliberately sunk for divers in

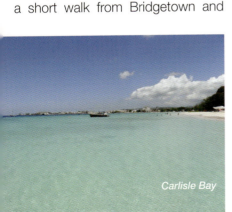

Carlisle Bay

1985 but the Pamir has faired better, remaining completely intact, while the Friar's Craig has broken into three large mangled pieces. None the less, they both provide excellent man-made reefs, hosting a multitude of marine creatures. In 2014 a freighter called the Brianna went down in the outer area of Carlisle Bay. However she has not been made safe for divers as yet.

Night diving is a thrilling addition to any of the day dives you may experience and all dive shops will offer this option. Night diving is a good time to see marine creatures that prefer to come out of the reef under the cover of darkness. For instance, you are more likely to see an octopus at night than during the day. Lobsters, shrimps, crabs, basket stars and crinoids all prefer to feed at night.

Fewer fish are out or 'awake' at night, but these fish can be found sleeping among the coral or just stationary and docile.

At night, octopus like this Caribbean reef one, come out and feed. Taken on the Pamir.

Almost all the dives in Barbados are drift dives, but this does not mean that strong currents prevail. It is merely easier and more enjoyable to continue diving in one direction, always seeing a new part of the reef, rather than going back over old ground.

A crinoid at night.

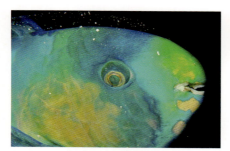

At night, Parrotfish secrete a mucus from their mouths, forming a protective cocoon that envelops the fish, possibly hiding its scent from potential predators. Scientists also believe the mucus is dis-tasteful to predators.

There is such a variety of diving experiences around Barbados, enough for any keen scuba divers or underwater photographers and we hope you leave contented but wanting to return for more.
Come back soon!

BARBADOS HYPERBARIC CHAMBER

CALL: 436-5483 or Dr Brown 230-9038

A hyperbaric chamber was installed in Barbados in 2004 and is operated 24/7 by a special health unit of the Barbados Defence Force (BDF). **Dr Brown** is one of the hyperbaric physicians and can be contacted regarding any diving medical issue. The chamber is situated in St. Ann's Fort, the Garrison. It is of vital importance that in any diving emergency, first make direct contact with the chamber or **Dr Brown** then the ambulance service.

Chamber's services are US$430.00/hour.

MULLINS BEACH BAR & GRILL
Mullins Beach   St Peter
T: (246) 422 2044

    tripadvisor

Serving Menu from 11am - 7pm
Live Music on Sunday evenings
5pm in season only
Parking: Street and Car Park

Mullins is the ultimate west coast beach bar offering inventive good quality food at affordable prices. Choose from modern classics, local twists, daily specials and a children's menu. They have an excellent wine list and plenty of skilled bar staff to serve from a great list of cocktails. Mullins is run by owners/managers Rory Rodger and Jason Hyndman, who have created a friendly relaxed atmosphere. The bar area provides several huge TV's to watch the latest sporting events from around the world throughout the day.

On Sundays at 5pm a local band plays "classic rock hits", the evening is very popular with both locals and visitors.
Mullins beach bar is one of the most popular places to have a sun-downer on the west coast; sit on the beach, the terrace or in the restaurant the view is the same - perfect.

Tiny delicate polyps of flower coral feeding at night.

BARBADOS DIVE CENTRES

All Barbados dive centres do their best to enhance environmental awareness among their divers. They do not indulge in or condone fish feeding, spear fishing (unless it's a Lionfish), riding of marine life or collection of shells or coral.

Barbados has five fully equipped independent dive centres which are located along the west coast and in Carlisle Bay. They can all provide scuba diving with gear rentals, PADI courses, transport and a professional safety conscious service. All the dive centres use aluminium tanks, provide weights and offer economical dive packages for those that intend to do multiple dives.

Barbados is the perfect island to furthering your scuba certification, with year round warm water and plenty of easy dives it couldn't be easier.

All the dive centres offer a range of PADI courses from Open Water, and Advanced up to (with prior arrangement) Instructor level. Especially popular now are courses for teenagers. Junior PADI courses start from age 10+ in the sea and Bubble maker is available from age 8+ in a pool. For anyone who just wants to have a look at what it's all about try a Discover Scuba dive. All the dive centres provide PADI Referral courses, which is when you complete the open water dives parts of the course in Barbados, to complete your certification. They also offer the Padi e-learning system where you can do all the classroom work online before you get to the island.

Squirrelfish by Lucy Agace

PRICES INCLUDING GEAR IN USD:
One tank dive range between
$63.00 - $75.00

10 dive packages range between
$475.00 - $510.00

Prices quoted in this book are correct at time of going to press and they may vary as time passes by.

There is also a good selection of speciality short courses such as: night diving, wreck diving, nitrox, deep dives and technical diving. Lucy Agace offers INON underwater photography 1-5 day courses, please see the BUPA advert on page 139. As a result of my experience, I know that every dive can be improved with a little foresight and local knowledge. If there is a particular creature you wish to see or photograph, just let the dive centre know; they will always do their best to accommodate requests. All the dive centres are accustomed to the needs of photographers. Extra help is often at hand to assist with the carrying of equipment.

In 2007 a professional divers organisation was formed called the Barbados Dive Operators Association (BDOA) which brings all the dive centers under one umbrella for marine life conservation, promotion, diving safety standards and general management of resources. This association is dedicated to ensuring the safety standards of local diving and the conservation of the marine ecology of Barbados. A number of the dive centres work with marine conservation foundations and charities such as: Beautiful Oceans, Scuba Trust, Reef Check, Padi Aware and offer further educational experiences in Coral Reef Biology.

Nitrox is currently available on the island from a few places, please look for the nitrox logo. Nitrox greatly extends bottom time which is hugely useful to the Barbados dive scene as many of the reefs are in the 60ft - 120 ft depth range.

Whilst I have listed 39 dive sites which the dive centres know very well, they also have a few special ones of their own; so please ask them for more details.

Most morning dives leave from 9:00am onwards and then carry on at intervals throughout the day. Afternoon dives operate anytime after 1:30pm. Times of course vary, and so always confirm dive times before booking. A soft drink is usually provided on the boat, but you can bring your own too. Dive centres do their best to accommodate their customers holiday spirit but you are advised not to drink heavily on the evening before a dive. Be smart, be safe. Apart from scuba diving gear most dive centres also hire wetsuits, snorkelling equipment and cameras. Transport to and from the dive centre is usually included in the price, but always arrange this with the dive operator. Entry onto a dive boat is mostly from the beach with the exception of Reefers & Wreckers who operate from the Port St Charles quayside.

Starting in the north going down the west coast, you will encounter the dive shops in this order: *Reefers and Wreckers, Hightide Water Sports, Rogers Scuba Shack, Barbados Blue Water Sports and West Side Scuba.*

REEFERS AND WRECKERS

TIMOTHY HOUSE, ORANGE ST, SPEIGHTSTOWN, ST. PETER

 (246) 422 5450
(246) 234 1377

 scubadiving@caribsurf.com
www.scubadiving.bb

 tripadvisor

PICK UP DROP OFF: Yes

BOAT ENTRY: Dock

Jamali, Phil, Archie, Hayden

Reefers and Wreckers is the most northerly dive shop and is located in the enviable quaint, historic Speightstown. Local brothers Phillip and Michael Mahy set up the business in 1993 with their father. Phillip, a PADI Instructor, now manages the dive centre and personally instructs all the PADI courses with his blend of Bajan rhythm and charm.

Reefers and Wreckers believe in providing a calm, comfortable, safety conscious environment for their customers to enjoy the underwater world.

Although they do not teach courses in a pool you are however, likely to see a turtle swim by whilst you are learning your basic techniques, off the beach at Port St Charles. Not a bad start! Phil offers courses that range from Discover Scuba to Divemaster. Phil takes pride in his work and always teaches at the pace of the student, never rushing and always patient.

Phil works with Archie, who has been with him for over 15 years. Archie is extremely good at spotting all kinds of marine life on the reefs, if you want to see something in particular ask him before the dive and he will gladly do his best. Bare in mind the marine creature needs to be a species known to inhabit the dive site in the first place!

Phil teaching new students

Reefers have one of the most spacious dive shops, with showers, a toilet, gear washing facilities and a large comfortable study room. There is also a bar area upstairs where you can relax after the dive and enjoy the see view whilst writing in your logbook. They sell t-shirts, books, rash guards and rent wetsuits and any scuba gear you may need.

Reefers and Wreckers run a fast, single hull, covered dive boat with twin 400hp engines and will take up to 16 divers comfortably. The boat always carries safety equipment, spare gear, snacks and beverages between dives. Reefers are one of the few dive shops where you can board the dive boat from a dock, they use port St Charles to do this. Bottles are carried to the boat for you so all you need to bring is your equipment. The pre-dive brief is always very informative and a buddy check is carried out afterwards. Divers and equipment are always helped back into the boat after the dive. Cameras are looked after with great care and they carry mask cleaning fluid on board.

They cover all the west coast as far down as the SS Stavronikita and are pretty much the only dive centre that dive Sharks Hole, plus they have a few other northern sites that you can ask them about. These sites are very much weather dependant. They are the closest to the famed Cement Pier dive site but government restrictions don't allow diving when there is a vessel docked. Most mornings they operate a two tank dive which leaves at 9:00am - each at a different location, and the first is usually the deepest. Reefers are happy to fit the dive plans around the desires of their customers whenever possible, ultimately they are a flexible dive shop.

ENDORSEMENT:
I took a Padi OW course with Phil in 2014 and I must say he was so patient with me I really felt very safe with him at all times. My daughter also trained with him the year before and loved it. Sydney Francis

PRICES INCLUDING GEAR IN USD:
Single dive $70, 2 tank dive $125, a 10 dive package $475 including equipment. Please contact us for prices if you have your own gear

COURSES IN USD:
Referral $ 275.00 OW $425 AOW $325.00 Divemaster $750.
Reefers can provide further training in deep, night and wreck diver courses all of which are $300 each.

DIVE HIGHTIDE WATER SPORTS

**CORAL REEF CLUB HOTEL
PORTERS   ST JAMES**

- +(246) 432-0931 or 2302890
  Toll Free: (800)513-5763
- www.divehightide.com
  info@divehightide.com
- tripadvisor

PICK UP DROP OFF: Yes
BOAT ENTRY: Beach

Gavin, Edwin and Martyn.

Dive Hightide is a PADI resort ideally located at the exclusive Coral Reef Club hotel in Holetown, adjacent to the Folkestone Marine Park. Established in 1993 Hightide is now operated by Gavin Smith and Martyn Norsworthy. Gavin, who is a Padi Divemaster, has been diving since the early 90's and Martyn has been a Padi Instructor since 1987.

Hightide is committed to providing divers with the kind of professionalism and personal service they expect from a first rate dive operation. By providing quality service to their guests, Hightide have become one of the most recognizable names in Barbados scuba diving. Their strength is the experience and continuity of their team. Led by Master Instructor, Edwin Blackman, who has been with them since 1996; their dive boat Captain Victor, since 1997 and Instructor Simron, since 2002.

Hightide offers diving with no crowds and can accommodate experienced divers with their own equipment, computers, cameras and equally novice or single divers who may wish to rent gear. Hightide is centrally located for easy access to all the

Edwin with a student

dive sites from the north of the island down to Carlisle Bay. They operate a 2 tank dive service at 9:00 and an afternoon dive leaves at 2.30pm.

Both Gavin and Martyn believe strongly in the responsibility of dive operators to respect the marine environment. Close working ties with the Barbados Sea Turtle Project, The University of West Indies Reef Watchers program and Folkestone Marine Park help to enhance their divers' experience. Participate in one of Hightides' famous 'turtle tagging' dives alongside the biologists of the Barbados Sea Turtle Project and see conservation in action.

ENDORSEMENT:
I had a wonderful week of diving with Hightide and was very happy with the level of service and dives they provided. Thank you!"
Bruce Jones
2014.

Hightide operate two very comfortable dive boats.

They have two large covered dive boats which offer excellent comfort and stability, with dry central consoles, storage, a camera bucket and mask cleaning service. Juice and water is served between dives. Staff are on hand to help set up your equipment, load it on the boat, and after your dive wash and stow your equipment, so you can relax and enjoy your holiday.

COURSES: They offer a wide range of Padi courses from Discover Scuba up to Dive Master, led by Master Instructor Edwin Blackman.

Students begin their courses in the on site pool and there is an air conditioned room for studying.

ROGER'S SCUBA SHACK

BAY STREET, CARLISLE BAY
BRIDGETOWN, ST MICHAEL

 (246) 436 3483

 www.rogersscubashack.com
info@rogersscubashack.com

 tripadvisor

PICK UP DROP OFF: Yes

Mark, Roger and George

Since 1998, Roger Hurley has managed and owned this PADI dive centre along with his two brothers Mark and George. This is a busy, well organised dive shop with helpful and well trained staff who can cater for both groups and individuals.

Mark, George, Brian, Nick, Amy, Mark, Roger.

Wether you are a beginner looking to learn or improve your diving skills, a seasoned veteran or just needing some guidance 'The Scuba Shack' is the perfect place to experience the best diving around the island and enhance your vacation.

They recently re-located to new spacious premises right on the beach in Carlisle Bay, on Bay St opposite St Patricks church. With the extra space at the front of the dive centre they can now offer drinks and food with 'Finally Michaels' beach bar facility. So after your dive why not stay and get to know the locals or write out your logbook, all under the protection of a large covered area. They fill their own tanks on site and have comfortable air conditioned training rooms. Younger students take their skills tests and training in a small onsite pool and adults take their courses in Carlisle Bay.

Trained instructors, teach a range of courses from Discover Scuba to Dive Master and offer many other specialities such as night diver, wreck diver and underwater naturalist. All courses are run by highly experienced instructors who have a conscientious and patient approach to diving.

at all times. To get onboard the boat a ladder is lowered in shallow water in Carlisle Bay where the shop is located and this is always supervised.

Roger's offers a personal service with no crowds and can accommodate experienced divers with equipment, computers, cameras and equally novice or single divers who may wish to rent equipment.

Besides Roger, Mark and George the staff includes Nicholas Hurley (assistant instructor) and Amy (dive master) who are both passionate about the underwater world and exploring it with their divers.

Roger's runs a fast propose built 36 foot dive boat called Phoenix which easily takes up to 15 divers. Onboard they carry safety equipment, water and spare gear. They have a dry storage area for your personal items and cameras are looked after

A two tank dive leaves at 9:30am each morning and afternoon dives on the Carlisle Bay wrecks leave around 2:30pm. Soft drinks are served between dives in the morning and the pre-dive talks are well rehearsed and informative. Transport to and from hotels is available and advanced booking is essential.

Nick helps a young student diver.

PRICES INCLUDING GEAR IN USD:
Single tank $70, 2 tank dive $120 10 dive package $500.

COURSES IN USD:
Padi Referral $275, OW $475, AOW $350, Rescue Diver $425. Lots of specialty courses are available

ENDORSEMENT:
Randy says *"I have dived here several times over the years and when my daughter was old enough, we didn't hesitate to get her certified with Roger - he is the best".*

BARBADOS BLUE WATER SPORTS

**HILTON HOTEL, NEEDHAMS POINT
PEBBLES BEACH, CARLISLE BAY, ST MICHAEL**

📞 (246) 434 5764

✉ info@divebarbadosblue.com
www.divebarbadosblue.com

f ⓞⓞ **tripadvisor**

PICK UP DROP OFF: Yes

FREE WIFI

Barbados Blue Watersports was recently featured on the BBC and received the PADI Green Star Award, is owned and operated by Marine Biologist/NAUI Instructor & PADI Master Scuba Diver Trainer-Andre Miller MSc. Andre 'the Bajan' specialises in coral restoration, coral nurseries, and coral transplantation throughout the Caribbean.

The crew.

The dive shop is located on the beautiful Hilton Hotel complex where any diver or snorkeler can enjoy the calm Carlisle Bay, or purchase a day pass from the Hilton for scrumptious lunch or an exotic spa treatment after a day of diving. Barbados Blue's great location, gives them easy access the islands best dive sites on the south and west coasts. Their house-reef has 5 shallow wrecks, and the Turtle Experience site is less than 1 km away. Valet Diving!

Barbados Blue run two boats; Aunty Jas, which is the fastest dive boat on island, and is ideal for small groups, or private island tours. They even race Jas over to their sister dive shop Ecodive Grenada in under 5 hours. The second boat Mellissa 2, is a covered motorised catamaran that can comfortably take 18 divers, and fruit and water are

ENDORSEMENT:
Thank you Barbados Blue for the great diving! Lionfish hunting, wreck diving in Carlisle Bay, great professional staff, comfortable dive boat, excellent diving never left us thinking about when we can get back to Barbados again.
Star D

Aunty Jas

served on all morning tours. All of our boats are powered by 4-Stroke Yamahas with Ultra Low Emissions. Even their mask cleaner and soap is phosphate free, and they recycle every single bottle and plastic bag. You will never have to lift scuba tanks or weights before or after you dive, and high-res digital cameras are rented daily.

All staff are trained medics as safety is their paramount concern, and their knowledgeable, organised, fun dive crew includes PADI Staff Instructor Robert, and Divemasters; Roger, Russell, Danny, and Isabel who know many of the reefs better than some

fish. Our boat captains Rah and Rod are ex-military, and free divers Ahanii and Kazii are training to become the youngest instructors when they turn 18.

Dive courses range from Bubble-maker for ages 8+ to PADI Assistant Instructor. Barbados Blue also run a wide range of environmental projects and internships for keen local youths.

PRICES INCLUDING GEAR IN USD:
Single dive $75, 2 tank dives $150, 10 dive package $510.

COURSES IN USD:
Discover Scuba $99 OW $460 AOW $375 Rescue $395
Specialty courses on request.

Barbados Blue have recently introduced UV (Ultra Violate Light) night diving which costs $120 including equipment. Barbados Blue will set you up with all the necessary equipment and guide you on a night dive with a difference. See the reef and marine life like never before.

Andre with a green turtle.   Hilton pool complex.   Andre instructing a young student.

Barbados Blue is a PADI FIVE star dive resort, therefore E-learning, finding lost cert cards, and immediate on-line certification reduces study time while in Barbados. This facility is a dealer for Cressi and Scubapro dive gear, so only the best gear is rented or sold, and there is a full service center off property. They also sell T-shirts, rash guards, fish ID cards, books, and snorkel and dive gear.

Barbados Blue is a **100% AWARE** eco-diving facility and that means that for every student they certify at any PADI level they make a donation to ocean protection with the **Project AWARE** foundation. They are also a PADI **Coral Watch Dive Operator**; as such they regularly monitor coral reefs and submit data to provide critical information on coral health issues. Barbados Blue is also the **Reef Check** Coordinating scuba diving shop for the Eastern Caribbean. They conduct educational seminars for schools, youth camps and organize underwater and beach clean-ups.

In addition to being a PADI Project AWARE Coral Reef Monitoring Dive Centre they host the Eastern Caribbean's Coral Reef Crime Scene Investigation (CSI) workshop.
Earning a **Green Star Award** demonstrates a dedication to conservation across a wide range of business functions, including (but not limited to):

- Conservation Leadership
- Waste generation and recycling
- Water conservation
- "Environmentally friendly" transportation practices
- Paperless interactions with their PADI Regional Headquarters
- Donation to Project AWARE

At present the shop is the hub for the **Saving Coral Reefs** project where souvenir wrist bands are sold for $5.00 and the proceeds of this project helps to import Lionfish culling equipment, community based coral reef monitoring, and replacing dive moorings.

OCEANSPORTS TECHNICAL DIVING (BARBADOS) LTD

Jim Driscoll LCDR US Coast Guard (Ret)
Christ Church, Barbados

 Bdos (246) 247 5893
USA (727) 643 6278

 www.ostechdive.com
jim@ostechdive.com

Oceansports Technical Diving (Barbados) Ltd specializes in personalized/private diver training and guided dives to suit all levels of experience, from an introductory scuba experience for the non-diver to technical, technical wreck, advanced Nitrox and Trimix.

Captain Jim Driscoll is the owner and principal instructor at Oceansports. He is retired from ~ 30 years active duty US Coast Guard service and has more than 45 years of diving & vessel operation experience. Jim is a NASE Instructor Trainer, IANTD Technical, Trimix & Rebreather Instructor, PADI/DSAT Tec Rec Deep, Trimix & Rebreather Instructor, PADI Master Scuba Diver Trainer, Emergency First Response Instructor, DAN Instructor and fully certified cave diver. He also holds a U.S. Merchant Marine 100-ton Master's License, a Barbados Speed Boat License, BS degree in Marine Engineering Technology & AS degree in Electrical Engineering Technology.

Jim is married to a Barbadian and spends his year split between Barbados and Florida where he operates Oceansports International, LC. He is the most experienced and knowledgeable scuba diver and instructor on Barbados. He assists with technical matters for the EALASS social dive club of Barbados and both he and his wife are active members of the club.

Jim can supply custom blended Nitrox, Normoxic & Hypoxic Trimix and a full range of deco gases (41%- 100% O2), rebreather tanks & absorbent. Complete back and side mount technical equipment outfits are also available for diving & training.

ENDORSEMENT:
*I took a PADI Enriched Air course with Jim and I found him to be a very thorough and patient instructor. I used Nitrox everyday whilst diving Indonesia recently which allowed me to make the most of my time there. Great course.
Lucy Agace 2011*

WEST SIDE SCUBA CENTRE

"MOWBRAY", HASTINGS MAIN ROAD, CHRISTCHURCH

 (246) 429 2109
Cell: (246) 262 1029

 www.westsidescuba.com
westsidescuba@gmail.com

 tripadvisor

PICK UP DROP OFF: On request
BOAT ENTRY: Beach/Dock

This is one of the most popular dive centres on the southern shores. They manage to mix warm Bajan hospitality with a top quality professional and personal service. At West Side nothing is too much trouble and they pride themselves on delivering a fun, safe and friendly diving experience whilst catering for all levels and requests. They are an Eco-Dive facility and keep in mind, at all times, the conservation of the reefs.

Owned and managed by Peter Grannum, a Padi MSDT Instructor since 1993, West Side Scuba Centre was set up in 1993 and is a Padi 5 star Golden Palm resort. West Side offer an extensive range of courses from Discover scuba to Dive Master. They can also provide further most specialist courses, please contact them for more details.

PADI instructors, Peter and G lead the daily dives and you will not find a more exuberant and relaxed team of professional, who's aim is to give you the best diving experience they can.

Liam, Peter, Roy and G

Peter and his team look for the best sites to dive on the day to suit divers' abilities and requests.

Peter and G, a Padi instructor, Dive Masters Liam and Roy assist on the dives, set you up with your equipment before you dive and wash it down afterwards. Tanks and weights are on the boat so there is no heavy carrying and help is always at hand. Your enjoyment is always of paramount importance to the West Side team.

West Side has a powerful 34 foot single hull boat called Jamie Too, which takes up to 12 divers with tanks safely stowed in racks. On every outing they carry full safety equipment, including O2 and spare diving gear. An informative dive brief takes place before everyone gets their gear on at the dive site. This usually includes useful instructions on currents, dive direction and what to look out for. In between dives they have refreshments of juice and water

ENDORSEMENT:
If you are going to dive in Barbados this is the place to book with! By far the best staff. March 2015 Andrea

and West Side Scubas' coconut bread to nibble on as you get ready for your next dive.

West Side Scuba has a daily two tank dive which leaves at 9:30am and the first dive is usually deepest. They visit the wreck of the SS Stavronikita once a week and cover all south coast dive sites and up the west coast as far as Dottins Reef dive site.

Each day at 2.00pm they have 1 tank and Discover Scuba dives which go to the lovely Carlisle Bay wrecks. Night dives are on request.
You can start your dive course at home by using their online Padi e-learning courses and by using West Side as your dive shop in Barbados. This way you can make the most of your holiday time on the island and spend more time underwater diving

They also stock a selection of snorkelling equipment, single use cameras and t-shirts, while larger cameras and wetsuits are available for rent.

PRICES INCLUDING GEAR IN USD:
Quoted in USD including equipment
Single tank dive $63, 2 tank dive $120, 10 dive package $500.

COURSES IN USD:
PADI OW $450.00, AOW $405, Dive Master $610, Referral $279.00.

This black urchin shrimp was found on the spines of a magnificent urchin which are regularly seen at the cement plant pier dive site.

BARBADOS
LIST OF DIVE SITES

1	SHARKS HOLE	P46
2	MAYCOCKS	P49
3	CEMENT PLANT PIER	P50
4	BRIGHT LEDGE	P55
5	PAMIR	P56
6	GREAT LEDGE	P61
7	THE FARM	P63
8	SPAWNEE	P65
9	WHITEGATES	P67
10	TROPICANA	P69
11	LONESTAR	P70
12	MERLIN BAY	P71
13	CHURCH POINT	P73
14	DOTTINS REEF	P75
15	SANDY LANE	P77
16	BOMBAS REEF	P79
17	FISHERMANS	P80
18	CRYSTAL COVE	P83
19	VICTOR'S REEF	P85
20	SS STAVRONIKITA	P86
21	BELL BUOY	P93
22	CLARKES BANK	P94
23	CARLISLE BAY WRECKS	P96
24	OLD FORT	P101
25	CASTLE BANK	P103
26	FRIARS CRAIG & RUM BARREL & ASTA REEF	P104
27	CARLEYNE	P109
28	PIECES OF EIGHT	P111
29	CARIBEE	P113
30	THE BOOT	P115
31	THE MUFF	P117
32	ST LAWRENCE REEF	P119
33	CLOSE ENCOUNTERS /DOVER	P121
34	HIGHWIRE	P123
35	MOUNT CHARLIE	P125
36	THE FINGER	P127
37	GRAEME HALL SHALLOWS	P129
38	THE STUDY	P131
39	RAGGED POINT	P133

SHARKS HOLE

1

LOCATION: North Coast
TYPE DIVE: Drift
SKILL LEVEL: Advanced

PHOTO TIP: Wide Angle
DEPTH: 60' - 95'

This is the most northern dive site and very susceptible to sea swells and choppy seas, which makes it a hard dive site to visit regularly or plan to dive. Steep rocky cliffs run all along the northern coastline, this formation continues underwater creating an unusual seascape of walls and massive boulders. It is well worth the effort.

All divers enter the water together and descend with the guide as a group. You will descend into a large sandy basin surrounded by walls at about 70ft. At one end there is a narrow opening, the 'hole' which leads to a passage through the rock and out to the other side.

A Nurse Shark rests on the bottom in the passage.

Elkhorn coral stands majestically on top of the reef.

Whilst you move through the narrow passage - try not to kick hard and disturb the sand - its here on the bottom where nurse sharks are often found resting. The passage is big enough to fit two divers at a time, so you will need to wait your turn to go through. This is one of the reasons Phil, from Reefers and Wreckers, only takes down a maximum of 6-8 divers.

You will exit the passage into a sandy area at 95 feet and continue the dive keeping the wall on your left. There are many large boulders piled up in some places and walls continue on both sides. The fish life varies all along here with small schools of Chub, Black Durgon and Black Jack.

The dive continues up over the walls across rock where the occasional sponges, sea fans and some corals have taken hold. This 'reef' gradually slopes up to about 35 ft and in this area don't miss the critically endangered elkhorn coral, it's stunning. This is a great place to end the dive and for gassing off.

Nurse shark face. By Henrietta Fastos.

MAYCOCKS

2

LOCATION: North West Coast
DIVE TYPE: Drift • Reef
SKILL LEVEL: Minimum Novice

PHOTO TIP: Wide Angle and Zoom
DEPTH: 50' - 130'

Unlike the west coast reef which runs parallel to the coastline, this reef runs perpendicular to the shoreline and covers a huge area, which is not possible to see on one dive. The northern side of the reef is broken-up by a number of deep sand channels, giving the dive a unique quality. Its northerly situation ensures that it is infrequently dived, thus safeguarding the reef's distinct attributes, but this also means when the sea is rough it is impossible to get to.

Entry is a free descent, down to 55 feet and during descent have a good look around at the spectacular view of this reef area. The reef slopes gently down on the left, where there are many beautiful clusters of branching antler sponge and big barrel sponges and then it drops away to over 150 feet. The deep sand channels are off to the right. The clarity of the water is usually good here and there is often a current which will take you in a north/westerly direction.

The dive continues along the sloping reef over beautiful formations of plate star coral, brain coral and orange elephant ear sponge, with sea plumes, sea fans, gorgonias, yellow tube and purple finger sponges are also in abundance. Fish life is good with many species of tropical reef fish, which include hogfish, rock beauties, brown chromis, squirrelfish and hamlets but none are abundant. Keep an eye out for blue headed wrasse cleaning stations and watch the creole wrasse come down for a quick clean.

The reef is broken up by some large sandy areas which are quite useful for photographers to set down. Turtles and rays can be found resting on these sand patches, they do make excellent photo opportunities. Lionfish hunters dive here whenever possible to keep the numbers down.

Gorgonias and branching antler sponge are a common reef feature on this dive.

CEMENT PLANT PIER

LOCATION: West Coast
DIVE TYPE: Shallow • Return
SKILL LEVEL: Minimum Novice

PHOTO TIP: Any lense
DEPTH: 24'

It's a well known fact that an abundance of marine life tends to congregate underneath piers. Due largely to the overhead cover it provides and the safety from various types of debris - large and small - that tends to end up there. But also we build these structures in areas protected from strong winds and turbulent seas and many species prefer to inhabit these relatively protected environments.

This is a fantastic 'critter hunt' dive whether you have a camera or not you could see almost anything. This is my favourite dive site, for many reasons but because it's so shallow, at 24 ft, I can last over 11/2 hours on one tank and so can take my time exploring the whole area, looking for critters to photograph. It's also a great wide angle dive site with the tall pillars and sunlight streaming down and the shallow depth means there is a lot of light for photography, even if you don't have strobes.

This is a large 'T' shaped pier with a long leg part and the top of the T section is supported by four smaller outer pillar sections and one huge central pillar area. The central area is where the cargo vessels moor up and if there is a boat there dive centres are not permitted to dive this site.

The dive usually starts on the southern end where the guides will lead their group around each pillar section showing you various critters as they find them. The highlight of this dive is the almost certainty of seeing a seahorse and they could be anywhere during the dive in any section, and not always on the ground. Each guide will have his special way

Emily watches an Octopus on a pillar.

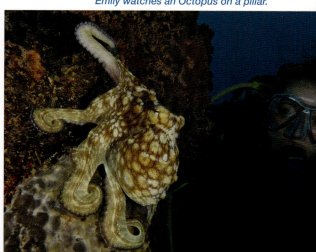

Henrietta looks at some amazing sponge growth.

There are a few large barrel sponges on the 'leg' section of the T, not too far down which can harbour all sorts of creatures; above this area is usually swarming with sergeant major fish. Octopus, white spotted filefish, trumpet fish and banded coral shrimp can also be found here.

Nearly all the giant pillars are covered in a profusion of brightly coloured tube and encrusting sponges. This is a good dive to take a torch down with you to illuminate the diversity of marine life. One of the pillars in the central section near the top, at the front, are covered in yellow cup coral which come out at night to feed but you can still see the colour during the day.

Fish of all kinds congregate under various parts of the pier and they vary during the year. I've seen massive schools of mackerel scads and schools of sennets and jack pass through. Small schools of yellow goat fish, blackbar soldier fish and French grunts live all year round in various places, but mainly in the central area. It is not unusual to see pelagic fish passing through looking for a quick meal either.

of guiding this dive but there is plenty of time to see all the pillar sections unless there is a strong current, which usually runs in a southerly direction.

An orange seahorse hides amongst orange sponge.

Sunlight under the central section.

Sailfin blennys and pike blennys are more often found on the southern inside part of the T, fairly near where it meets the leg part but down on the sand. These blennies are very small, at the most about two inches long. Sailfin blennies are often here in pairs and when one darts out of its hole and "dances" about 15 feet away you might see another one do the same. If you want to try and photograph them you are in for a long wait. I suggest that you don't get too close, or they will not come out at all, use a zoom lens if possible and you will

Frogfish are very unusual looking fish with a round shaped body and short thick fins that look like webbed feet. They sit motionless, with a transparent fishing rod like appendage sticking up above the mouth. This is to attract unsuspecting small fish close to its mouth so that it can be gulped down. This beguiling creature is not going to win a beauty contest but it is none the less an amazing sight. I noticed that although he sits in one spot for some time he is very aware of his surroundings. When they do move they sort of hop/jump along the reef, hence their name!

need a DSLR camera. I have tried with a compact and the focus time lag is

The lure of this Longlure yellow frogfish is clear to see. Photo by Henrietta Passos.

A well camouflaged Bottlenose Batfish.

the furthest north pillar section. It is very hard to find because there is a large area of sand in-between. This small reef has good sponge growth and lots of reef fish but the real reason to dive it would be to find the rare Bottlenose Batfish (see photo). Pretty impossible to see unless they move as they are so well camouflaged. They have a tiny stick thing which protrudes just under their extended 'nose' which, it is thought, they wiggle about to attract food (see photo p21).

too slow to freeze the frame.

Jawfish are amazing creatures that incubate their eggs in their mouth! This would make eating during this time impossible, hence they must eat a few eggs. The eggs develop quite quickly and the jawfish actually tosses the eggs in its mouth during this period, it's amazing to watch. Jawfish usually produce eggs in January and during this time they don't tend to disappear down their burrows, providing great photo opportunities. Found anywhere here, in burrows in the sand, look for small round groups of finger coral.

There is also a patch reef, rarely visited, off the pier to the west - from

There are masses of magnificent sea urchins here but they move around.

Be careful during every part of this dive as there are lots of very well camouflaged scorpionfish lying anywhere around and their spines are excruciatingly painful if touched. (see photo P61)

By no means any less interesting you may also see the following marine life; turtles, flying gurnards, smooth trunkfish, palometa, barracuda, tarpon, chromis, spotted eel, peacock flounder, french angel fish, sand diver, puffer fish, balloon fish, scrawled filefish, gray triggerfish, spotted drum, pipefish and sharptail eels.

Yellow cup coral by Henrietta Passos.

BARBADOS DIVE GUIDE

DIVE SITES

Cement Plant Pier

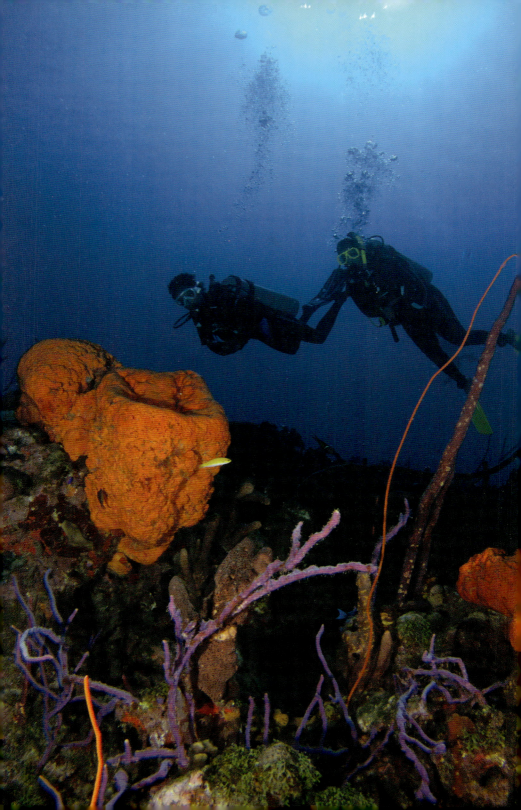

BRIGHT LEDGE 4

LOCATION: West Coast
DIVE TYPE: Drift • Reef • Night
SKILL LEVEL: Minimum Novice

PHOTO TIP: Wide Angle
DEPTH: 60' - 120'
BUOY: Yes

This dive site is located right out from the jetty at Port St Charles and only dived by Reefers and Hightide because of its northerly location. Bright Ledge is part of the fringing reef that runs along the west coast, and the top of the reef is 60 feet deep and about 60 feet across. It is possible to see both edges of the reef drop away. The seaward side has a steep slope (not a wall), reaching down to 150 feet plus, while the inner side shelves to 140 feet. It is possible to dive in a northerly or southerly direction, depending on the direction of the current, and southerly dives will last longer as the reef continues at a depth of 60 feet for much longer.

This is a very popular dive site and gets its name from the spectacular array of brightly coloured corals, sponges and fish life found here. There is yellow, purple, orange and green sponge in all areas of the reef. On close inspection the green finger sponge is covered in tiny bright yellow polyps, called golden zoanthids, which look a bit like mini suns.

This undulating reef comprises a variety of hard corals balanced with soft corals and sponges, the richness of which is not found anywhere else. It is best to travel across the reef slowly so as not to miss the squirrelfish, lizardfish, rock beauties, hogfish, turtles, parrotfish, white spotted filefish and barracudas, to name just a few of the species you will see.

There are numerous giant barrel sponge formations along the way and you more than likely see turtles, especially to the north.

The further south you get you will notice the coral growths seem to get bigger and more concentrated. I often leave this dive reluctantly and wish they could set the buoy in a more southerly position.

Mandisa and Danielle enjoying the reef.

THE PAMIR 5

LOCATION: West Coast
DIVE TYPE: Wrecks • Reef • Return • Night
SKILL LEVEL: Minimum Novice

PHOTO TIP: Any Lens
DEPTH: 40' - 50'
BUOY: Yes

The Pamir is a 170 ft freighter that was modified for diving and then purposely sunk in 1985. She dutifully came to rest upright in a shallow sandy area, perfect for beginner divers, second-tank and night dives. The bow, which lies at 40 ft, faces the beach while the curved stern is firmly buried in sand in about 50 ft. The mooring line is attached to the bow at 30 ft and this is also a good area to hangout before you ascend.

The hull of the Pamir has many large holes so divers can enter and exit with ease and the internal fittings have been removed so there is very little for diving equipment to snag on. The entire wreck is covered with encrusting sponges of various colours. Black coral and many sea fans have attached themselves to the hull on the port side of the stern and

Brian explores the stern of the Pamir.

Black coral grows on the bridge and one window is still intact.

wreck are perfect for them to lay their purple egg clusters on, which they seem to do throughout the year. As soon as the eggs are laid the mating pair spends every waking moment protecting their potential offspring from hungry fish, even their own species.

there is a huge old-fashioned anchor lies upright in the sand at the bow.

This is a perfect wreck to 'cut your teeth on' if you have never dived a wreck before, but equally, there is a lot to see and explore for the experienced diver too. The bridge is quite large and open with one surviving window at the front, which is surrounded by an orange coloured black coral bush. And if you are caught short there is a porcelain toilet on the bridge, but sorry, no door! Because of the large holes in the hull there is plenty of light inside the wreck, which means there is no need to carry a torch. However a torch light does come in handy if you want to see the true brilliance of the coloured sponges and invertebrates which have taken over the ship.

In the central area there is a large open cargo hold where it is possible to see grunts, blackbar soldierfish, trumpet fish, and sergeant major fish which shower the wreck. The sergeant major fish are a well known attraction of the wreck, and they provide excellent photographic subjects. The flat surface walls of the

French angel fish feeds on sergeant major eggs. By Henrietta Passos.

There is a large window in the centre of the cargo hold which is home to spiny lobster, banded coral shrimps and feather dusters. Below this structure in the large man hold lies a huge, pink tentacled anemone with cleaner shrimp living in it. Be careful not to disturb the bottom particles, as they take a long time to settle back!

Bar Jacks and sergeant majors above the Pamir.

Pelagic fish such as spanish mackerel, barracuda and bar jack can often be seen cruising the wreck and reef area.

You may also see another strange fish called a flying gurnard. They are not often found swimming around but they frequent the sea bed in search of food. These fish are about 12 inches long; they have large eyes and mottled brown backs and are relatively unattractive. However when they extend their wings out they are totally transformed as their six-inch wings are a mesmerising luminescent blue/green colour.

Popping their heads up from the sand along the port side of the wreck is a colony of garden eels. If approached carefully, crouching on the sand, it is possible to get within a few feet of them. Seahorses have also been found in this area.

The surrounding reef is in good condition and supports a multitude of marine life. I found 2 rare red heart urchins,

Flying Gunard.

A beautiful tube anemone at night. By Henrietta Passos.

it's fairly shallow and you can look for creatures that inhabit reefs and wrecks on one easy dive. In the sand on the port side have a look for tube anemones, they are exquisitely beautiful.

burrowed in the sand. Also there are 4 species of sea anemones, on and around the wreck, and inhabiting them at least 2 species of shrimp - all perfect for macro photography. If you look closely you can find beautiful lettuce leaf slugs and brightly coloured fire worms, crawling across the reef.

Since the last book the authorities have added a new feature, a small 'Yellow Submarine' which lies off the port side of the bow to the left about 20 meters away. With good visibility you can see it from the front of the wreck.

If you want to do a night dive the Pamir is an excellent choice,

Fireworms. By Henrietta Passos.

Watch out for octopus, slipper lobsters, shrimps, eels and sleeping fish and be careful with your buoyancy so as not to harm anything.

The yellow submarine.

59

GREAT LEDGE   6

LOCATION: West Coast
DIVE TYPE: Drift • Reef
SKILL LEVEL: Minimum Novice

PHOTO TIP: Wide Angle
DEPTH: 55' - 100'

Situated just south of Speightstown, this site is similar to Bright Ledge. The reef begins at 50 feet and slopes down quite gently on the seaward side to great depths. While the land side is a steeper slope the water is often murky. The undulating reef top is covered in hard and soft corals. Most notable are the many branching antler sponges. They reach up from the reef like leafless trees.

Visiting this reef is like taking a walk through a garden with red gorgonias, purple sea fans, black coral bushes and sea plumes, all of which resemble the earthly plants and bushes we are accustomed to.

Once again, the dive can be led to the north or south, depending on the current if there is one. A southerly direction is preferable as the reef top stays at a dive-able depth of 65 feet for longer.

There seems to be a lot of fish action here. Hundreds of chromis and creole wrasse swarm the upper waters, constantly on the move. These school of fish look so graceful when, in one sweeping movement, they swerve together to miss the striking attack of a large cero or spanish mackerel. On the edge of the outer reef there is a good chance to see a passing school of atlantic spade fish. This large, round-shaped silver fish with black vertical stripes has a rather shimmering, ghost-like quality as it moves.

Lizardfish, soldierfish, scrawled filefish, trumpet fish and scorpion fish can all be found along the dive.

Scorpion fish.

Lower down, in between the coral and rock, spotted eels poke their heads out to look for passing food. They are relatively easy to approach but wagging fingers can be intrusive and may resemble food to them, so be careful.

Branching Antler sponge and Squirrel fish.

THE FARM 7

LOCATION: West Coast
DIVE TYPE: Circular Reef• Drift
SKILL LEVEL: Minimum Advanced

PHOTO TIP: Any Lens
DEPTH: 60' - 80'

The Farm is an unusual dive site because the reef is a circular shape. The reef reaches approximately 100 feet across and gently slopes down to 90 feet or more on all sides. Because it is separated from the fringing coastal reef, it often has a current running across it which in turn provides ample food for the abundant marine life. There is no buoy here so the dive begins with a free descent to 60 feet; the highest part of this fairly flat reef.

Covered in hard and soft corals, the reef is home to many fish such as scrawled filefish, damselfish, spotted drums, trunkfish and several varieties of parrotfish. Welcomed visitors at the time of our dive were several yellow snappers, an uncommon reef fish.

The Farm is another dive where turtles are likely to be seen. If you find a turtle on the reef take care to approach it slowly. Once it takes off don't head strait for it but travel alongside it in the same direction. You may be rewarded when the turtle swims with your group rather than away from it.

Green finger, orange elephant ear, lavender finger and lumpy finger sponge are all common here but what stands out on the reef are the yellow tube sponge clusters.

Large expanses of flat star coral also support a variety of colourful christmas tree worms and there are some lovely ball shaped brain corals.

A creole wrasse passes a yellow tube sponge cluster.

Lucy finds a huge, resting hawksbill turtle. By Henrietta Passos.

SPAWNEE

8

LOCATION: West Coast
DIVE TYPE: Reef • Return
SKILL LEVEL: Minimum Novice

PHOTO TIP: Any Lens
DEPTH: 50' - 80'

This is a wide reef with a relatively flat top at 50 feet, which gets wider the further north you travel. There is a mooring buoy and rope to descend down to the reef and unless there is a current you will be led back to the rope to ascend from the dive.

This is a vibrant reef, covered in an assortment of hard and soft corals and some big yellow tube sponge clusters which make great subjects for photos. I also found a beautiful delicate red sea whip which looks brown and boring until you shine a light on it, they are not widely seen in Barbados.

The fish life is diverse and plentiful on this reef, with schools of yellow goatfish, hamlets, hogfish and princess parrotfish. It is possible to find blennies on the hard coral surfaces and feather dusters or tube worms.

Large schools of creole wrasse, boga fish and chromis pass overhead throughout the dive. They spend most of the time in the shallow water levels between the surface and reef, but occasionally come down and visit cleaning stations. Cleaning stations are common reef features throughout the world and a limited number of fish perform the duty. In the Caribbean the bluehead wrasse otherwise known as the 'cleaner' wrasse, a small blue and green fish takes on the task. They get a good meal whilst the other larger fish have parasites removed from their bodies.

A group of bluehead wrasse, the yellow ones are juveniles. By Henrietta Passos.

Red Sea Whip.

BADASS'N DIVE CLUB
W: www.badassn.com
E: admin@badassn.com

If you have recently moved to, or are planning an extended stay in Barbados and love SCUBA diving, you should consider joining the Barbados Dive Association (BADASS'n). We are a friendly, non – profit club, that welcomes anyone with a love of diving, a respect for the island, its marine life and its party spirit. We encourage safe, affordable, fun recreational diving.

Over the past 25 years the club has grown from just a few people, to a membership of 50 or more with members from all walks of life and nationalities and a healthy mix of men and women, local and non-local. Club dives are weekly through out the year, using different dive operators and a wide variety of sites around the island.

You don't need to have lots of diving experience to join the club, in fact many new members only have done a handful of dives, but you do need to hold a dive certification by a recognized dive organization. The club actively encourages members to continue their interest in diving education and expand their knowledge about the marine environment both formally through courses and informally through the breadth of knowledge shared by club members.

As a member you can dive as little or as much as you like and the Club provides a great environment for meeting like-minded people. Our members have a broad array of interests including photography and videography, wreck diving, reef management, lionfish hunting, along with just having a good time! The financial benefits of membership are great too as members benefit from negotiated local rates, along with discounts off dive equipment bought locally.

The club has a number of social activities, which friends and family can join in too. These include, catamaran cruises, educational seminars, visiting historic sites, Segway tours, special events, BBQ's and parties!

There are several membership options which you can explore at our website:
www.badassn.com

WHITEGATES 9

LOCATION: West Coast
DIVE TYPE: Drift • Reef
SKILL LEVEL: Minimum Novice

PHOTO TIP: Any Lens
DEPTH: 55' - 80'
BUOY: Yes

This dive site lies between Spawnee and Tropicana on the same west coast barrier reef, and enjoys similar features. The buoy is situated at the north end of the reef so the dive has to go in a southerly direction regardless of the current. The reef is no more than 40 feet across and slopes down deeper the further south you travel. As a result, bottom time becomes shortened.

It is perhaps for this reason that Whitegates is dived less often than its two neighbours. However, there is still plenty to see so perhaps this dive is best suited to photographers who do not wish to travel great distances on a dive.

There are some very large barrel sponge growths that stand out on the reef, along with a few sea fans and good overall coral growth. The outer edge slants down quite abruptly in places giving photographers a chance to get the sun in a wide-angle reef shot. The reef fish are not as plentiful as the creole wrasse and chromes that spend most of their time in the water above the reef.

Sand divers, scorpion fish, turtles and eels are around, and on the reef's outer edge atlantic spadefish and tarpon have been seen.

Suzie hovers by a huge barrel sponge.

TROPICANA

10

LOCATION: West Coast
DIVE TYPE: Drift • Reef
SKILL LEVEL: Minimum Novice

PHOTO TIP: Any Lens
DEPTH: 60' - 80'

Tropicana is part of the reef that runs all the way down the west coast. The top of the reef varies between 50 and 70 feet in depth with drop-offs on either side going down to 130 ft. Divers are not usually led down the sides as the tropical marine life is plentiful on top and deeper diving restricts bottom time. The dive leader will decide which way to travel on the dive once the current's direction is assessed.

The dive site is named after the abundance of colourful sponges and fish that inhabit the reef. Finding a turtle is more a certainty than a possibility, and spotted eels are common too.

Watch out for the elusive scorpionfish; although quite small, the spines on their back deliver a venomous sting. Approach with caution, but don't panic if you see one. They only extend their dorsal spines when something attacks them, an inquisitive diver should not constitute a threat. They remain motionless on the bottom for reasonably long lengths of time and only move when closely approached. They can be considered excellent close-up photography material. (see p 61).

Lizard fish which are also seen here and on most reefs, have similar characteristics but without the venomous spines.

There are some very pretty soft corals dotted along this dive which are home for fish such as; trumpet fish, glasseye snappers and squirrel fish.

Phil from Reefers and sea plumes.

LONESTAR   11

LOCATION: West Coast
DIVE TYPE: Drift • Reef
SKILL LEVEL: Minimum Novice

PHOTO TIP: Macro & Close-up lenses
DEPTH: 30' - 40'

This dive site is situated opposite the restaurant called Lonestar, which lies between Holetown and Speightstown. It is also very near the area where the glass bottom boats bring people to see turtles. This is an easy dive and the reef is not susceptible to currents, so ideal for beginners and those that want a slow paced dive.

The mooring is in 30 feet on a sandy flat bottom with a number of small coral mounds dotted around. The coral growth gets more abundant as you travel west or north. The location at the beginning of the dive is not very inspiring, it is often used for diver training. But don't despair, the dive progresses north where the reef deepens and a wealth of unusual marine life can be found. Atlantic squid, spotted eels, burrfish, pufferfish, large coral crabs, scorpionfish, eagle rays, frogfish and seahorses are all on the reef - you just have to spot them.

The reef gently slopes down to the left, if you are travelling north and yellow, orange and green sponges add colour. Keep a look out in the sandy areas for the holes of the jawfish. They tend to arrange a few bits of dead coral around the edge of their burrows and sit with their heads just poking out. This is a dive to be taken slowly whilst having a close look in all the nooks and crannies.

Every time this site is dived something interesting will undoubtedly be seen.

Banded Jawfish with eggs in its mouth.

MERLIN BAY

12

LOCATION: West Coast
DIVE TYPE: Drift • Reef
SKILL LEVEL: Minimum Novice

PHOTO TIP: Zoom or Macro
DEPTH: 30' - 70'

A Red Coral Crab feeding on a piece of starfish by Henrietta Passos.

This reef is an extension of the Lonestar reef, which is largely covered in long, thick columns of lobed star coral interspersed with sandy areas. With no buoy, this dive site is only accessible to divers capable of making a free descent. The reef is only 25 feet deep at the start and is usually visible from the surface, making descent more achievable. There are a number of large finger coral mountains, a common inner reef characteristic of the west coast.

The reef starts flat and as the dive continues in a southerly direction, begins to slope gently down to 60 feet or more. Here the corals and sponges become less extensive and less sizeable.

It is likely that one will see turtles and sting rays anywhere along the dive, but especially lying on the sand next to or under coral mounds. Amongst the hard and soft corals there is always a chance to see spotted eels and crabs, and the usual tropical reef fish are everywhere. This is a good dive for photography as there are plenty of large sandy areas to settle down on to take photos. Thus making sure no corals are damaged.

Merlin Bay is an excellent dive location for novices and divers that prefer shallow water, but you may need to work hard to search for marine creatures yourself.

CHURCH POINT 13

LOCATION: West Coast
DIVE TYPE: Circular Reef • Drift
SKILL LEVEL: Minimum Novice

PHOTO TIP: Zoom & Close-up
DEPTH: 30' - 50'

Situated between the dive sites of Dottins and Merlin Bay, and incorporating many of their characteristics, Church Point is a large circular reef patch measuring over 100 feet across. The outer edges slope gently down and the reef just fizzles out in most sections. There is currently no buoy so a free descent is necessary and it's possible to dive either way around, depending on the direction of the current, if there is one.

There are masses of large and small hard corals interspersed with sandy areas, have a good look around these for corals for the smaller reef creatures.

Tall soft corals, green finger and yellow tube sponges are scattered around the reef. The large sandy areas attract sting rays and it is possible to get quite close when they are lying on the sand.

There is just about every variety of common reef fish here in plentiful supply, including black durgon fish - a typical sign of a healthy reef. Scrawled and white spotted filefish, grunts and butterfly fish are easily visible, while moray eels, octopus and turtles are more challenging to find.

This dive site is usually used as a second morning dive, because it's nice and shallow. For a photographer it would be an ideal time to change to a close-up or macro lens because this type of protected reef allows photographers to find and get close-up to small subjects. In addition, the sand provides a solid base to set down on and not damage the reef. This dive site would also make a perfect spot for a night dive.

A young Balloonfish. By Henrietta Passos.

A spotted eel gets attention from a cleaning goby. By Henrietta Passos.

DOTTINS REEF 14

LOCATION: West Coast
DIVE TYPE: Drift • Reef
SKILL LEVEL: Minimum Novice

PHOTO TIP: Any Lens
DEPTH: 40' - 70'
BUOY: Yes

The mooring buoy for Dottins is anchored at 40 feet, the rope leads you onto a fairly flat sandy reef area. As you make your way south/westwards the reef slopes away on your right to 70 feet or more.

This is a beautiful mainly flat large reef and as you carry on south the reef breaks up and there are large areas of sand and huge coral mountains. A large school of sennet fish inhabit the reef further south and you are more likely to see turtles here. There is a lot to see on this dive so try to keep moving and save some bottom time for the south.

The early part of this reef has countless sea plumes and sea whips and in some places it feels like one is floating through an underwater forest of trees. They provide a natural hiding place for trumpet fish and a red fish called the glasseye snapper. Foureye Butterfly fish can be seen in pairs and sometimes as many as eight darting from one sea plume to the other - feeding.

Dottins is not short of fish. As you descend then it is possible you will pass through large schools of blue and brown chromis feeding on the passing food. There are plenty of scrawled filefish, peacock flounder, trumpet fish, parrotfish, angel fish, clown wrasse, threespot damselfish and, with a keen eye, spotted drums and mantis shrimp can be seen. Fabulous yellow tube sponge and purple finger sponge add vibrant colour to the reef. Some huge towering barrel sponge structures stand out, which give a welcome refuge to small fish and banded coral shrimp.

The face of a peacock flounder. By Henrietta Passos.

Sea plumes and foureye butterfly fish.

SANDY LANE   15

LOCATION: West Coast
DIVE TYPE: Drift • Reef
SKILL LEVEL: Minimum Novice

PHOTO TIP: Any Lens
DEPTH: 40' - 90'
BUOY: Yes

This dive site is located on the barrier reef opposite the beautiful bay where the famous Sandy Lane Hotel stands in Holetown. The mooring line is tied to the top of the reef at a depth of 60 feet and the dive can travel to the north or south. The direction of the dive will depend on the current, which is only assessable when at the mooring. The reef deepens as you travel south while the north gets shallower between 40 and 50 feet. Similar to most of the barrier reef sites it is dome shaped with fairly abrupt slopes on both sides. The outer edge goes down to below 100 feet where the corals give way to sand.

Descending the line will almost certainly take you through clouds of boga and creole wrasse. The reef top is undulating where sea plumes, gorgonias, sea fans and tall sponge clusters stand out. This growth density makes it difficult to set down to take photographs. Add to this the position of the sun directly overhead and it becomes quite impossible to take wide angle shots of the reef with the sun in - unless, of course, you can dive up-side down!

Both north and south directions have a generous selection of reef fish and pelagic fish such as bar jacks and mackerel pass along the dive usually along the outer edge. Barracuda, in small groups or on their own, can also be found hovering over the corals. The overall impression is one of activity and colour, for there's never a dull moment. Oh, and watch out for a large green moray eel.

A tiny triplefin blenny sits on valley brain coral.

Green moray eel with two cleaning gobies.

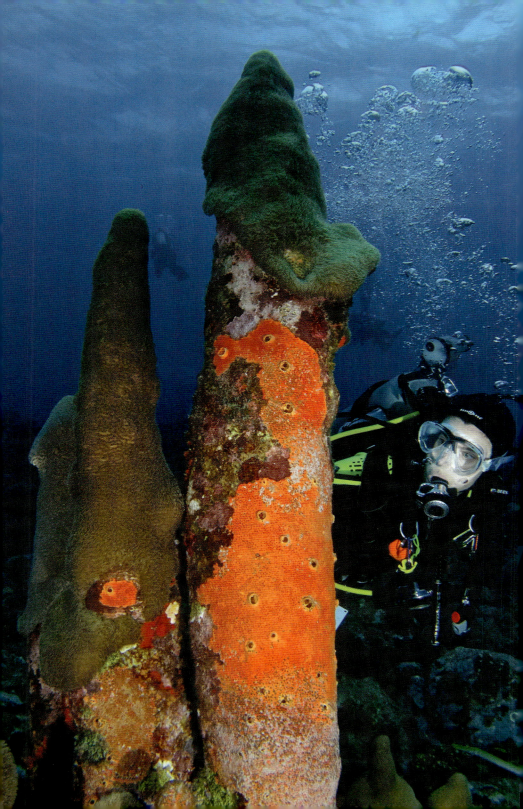

BOMBAS REEF   16

LOCATION: West Coast
DIVE TYPE: Drift • Reef
SKILL LEVEL: Minimum Novice

PHOTO TIP: Any Lens
DEPTH: 30' - 60'

This reef is located off Paynes Bay and was named after Bombas Beach Bar which has moved up the west coast just north of Mullins beach.

The mooring line brings you onto a flat sandy area at 30 feet scattered with small rock and coral boulders. The whole area is a mixture of broken coral, sand and healthy hard and soft corals. Moving west the reef gently slopes away where coral growth increases and barrel sponges and gorgonias are common.

Several tall pillar coral colonies, which are not common in Barbados, are scattered throughout the dive. For a hard coral they have particularly long polyp tentacles. Take a close look at the tentacles because they are usually out all the time, rather than just at night. They make great macro images.

A significant feature of this dive are the ten or more impressive giant cities of branching coral reaching twenty feet across and six feet high. Although some show signs of damage, most likely from wave turbulence and heavy anchors, they are still intact and a wonderful sight to see. Look for tube worms and crabs in-between the small coral tips.

The usual common reef fish, such as parrotfish, hogfish, chromis and squirrelfish can be found, but not in as great a quantity as on some other reefs. There is, however, plenty of feather dusters - a type of tube worm which is a good photographic subject. They vary in size and colour.

The area is known for eagle rays, turtles, spotted eels, spiny lobsters and snake eels. Lower down on the reef have a look for anemones, which often have tiny shrimp inside, or arrow crabs.

Arrow crabs and a juvenile scorpion fish shelter in the spines of a sea urchin.

Henrietta surveys the pillar coral.

FISHERMANS   17

LOCATION: West Coast
DIVE TYPE: Drift • Reef
SKILL LEVEL: Minimum Novice

PHOTO TIP: Any Lens
DEPTH: 45' - 80'
BUOY: Yes

Fishermans is on the outer reef at Paynes Bay and is a smaller version of Bright Ledge. The reef is a long dome shaped structure about 60 feet across with steep drop-offs on either side. The undulating reef top varies between 45 feet and 55 feet deep and is thickly covered in hard and soft corals with no space at all to set down. The dive can set off in a north or south direction depending on the current and there is a good variety of marine life to see; so take your time and make this a nice long leisurely dive.

To start with there are large sea fans and gorgonias that add a touch of height and colour to the reef and they often attract groups of two or three squirrelfish at their base. Lizardfish, peacock flounders and scorpionfish

A creole wrasse school passing over the reef.

A group of spotlight and striped parrotfish move across the reef feeding.

can be seen resting on the reef waiting for a meal to swim too close and blackbar soldierfish and yellow goatfish congregate low down on the reef.

Spotlight and princess, the more common of the parrotfish, are occasionally seen in groups and it is actually possible to hear them biting the hard coral - such is the power of their jaws. Have a good look around in the depths of the coral where the more shy creatures are lurking, for instance spider crabs and arrow crabs. Creole wrasse come down to the reef from their usual mid water area to visit cleaning stations. They always do this in a long streaming line, once one starts the others follow. They don't stay down for long a matter of minutes then stream back up again.

There is an abundance of orange, purple, antler, green and yellow sponges, but none growing particularly large.

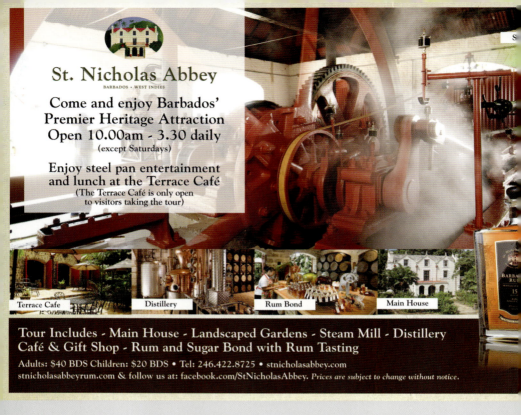

St. Nicholas Abbey
BARBADOS · WEST INDIES

Come and enjoy Barbados' Premier Heritage Attraction
Open 10.00am - 3.30 daily
(except Saturdays)

Enjoy steel pan entertainment and lunch at the Terrace Café
(The Terrace Café is only open to visitors taking the tour)

Terrace Cafe — **Distillery** — **Rum Bond** — **Main House**

Tour Includes - Main House - Landscaped Gardens - Steam Mill - Distillery Café & Gift Shop - Rum and Sugar Bond with Rum Tasting

Adults: $40 BDS Children: $20 BDS • Tel: 246.422.8511 • stnicholasabbey.com
stnicholasabbeyrum.com & follow us at: facebook.com/StNicholasAbbey. Prices are subject to change without notice.

Come and join Pamela in her Anusara inspired yoga classes with a focus on good alignment, breath, awareness and enhancing health and joy.

Pamela and her small team have created a light airy space for you to de-stress, keep fit and healthy or maintain your dynamic yoga practice whilst visiting Barbados. Experience the delight of a range of drop in and regular creative classes, styles and levels, designed to rejuvenate, harmonise and balance your mind and body.

SUNSHINE KULA YOGA
Highbury House, Sandy Lane, Holetown, St James.
T: 231 4468 or 432 8509
E: pamela@sunshinekula.com
W: www.sunshinekula.com

CRYSTAL COVE 18

LOCATION: West Coast
DIVE TYPE: Drift • Reef
SKILL LEVEL: Minimum Novice

PHOTO TIP: Macro & Close-up lenses
DEPTH: 25' - 60'

This dive site is situated just off the beach from the Crystal Cove Hotel in St James. The reef is quite flat and is not prone to currents, making it an ideal place to bring novices and students on a diving course.

The dive starts in only 25ft and moves along in a northerly direction from the buoy rope, with the reef sloping gently downwards out to sea on your left. Many large and small coral boulders are scattered over the seabed, containing a multitude of small marine creatures, such as banded coral shrimp, christmas tree worms and pipefish. Some large yellow and purple tube sponges give height and colour to the reef, check inside the yellow ones for small shrimp.

At the early stage of this dive, in the flat shallow area, it is possible to see many small groups of French and smallmouth grunts. They tend to congregate low on the reef using the coral as protection from predators. As with many of the other dives it is common to see hamlets, squirrelfish, yellow goatfish, striped parrotfish, blue tang, spotted trunkfish and foureye butterfly fish, to name a few. Keep your eyes open and scan in all directions, as turtles, rays, eels and squid have been regularly spotted on this dive.

Two banded coral shrimp in a barrel sponge.

VICTOR'S REEF 19

LOCATION: West Coast
DIVE TYPE: Drift • Reef
SKILL LEVEL: Minimum Novice

PHOTO TIP: Wide Angle & Close up
DEPTH: 50' - 80'

The top of the reef starts at 50 feet and slants down quite abruptly on the seaward side to 200 feet. This dive is pretty much like the other west coast ones, so depending on the direction of the current, the dive guide will go north or south along the reef. A wealth of hard corals that include star, brain, lettuce and pitted coral, vie for space on the seabed, there remains little or no space to settle on the bottom to take a photo. There are plenty of giant feather dusters and christmas tree worms growing out of these hard coral boulders.

Many tall clusters of purple and yellow tube sponge give the reef depth and colour, while the delicate feather-like branches of sea plumes and sea whips add softness to the overall appearance of the reef.

Various species of butterflyfish, French angel fish and Spanish hogfish pass by. Squirrelfish and blackbar soldierfish can be found hiding under coral and sometimes above, but they rarely venture far from their chosen 'living spaces'.

Seahorses can be found on many of the Barbados reefs, but they are very difficult to find. Here's a tip: they are nearly always close to the seabed, usually with their tail wrapped around a finger sponge or a strand of soft coral. More often than not they are motionless, making them doubly hard to see.

A yellow longnose seahorse clings to purple finger sponge. By Henrietta Passos.

Blackbar Soldier fish huddle by a sea rod.

SS STAVRONIKITA

Be warned, do not penetrate the wreck unless you are qualified to do so.

20

LOCATION: West Coast
DIVE TYPE: Wreck
SKILL LEVEL: Minimum Advanced
PHOTO TIP: Wide Angle
DEPTH: 25' - 135'
BUOY: Yes

The ultimate wreck dive in Barbados, the SS Stavronikita stands tall and proud as the biggest and best of an excellent selection of coastal ship wrecks. Although a mighty 365 feet long, lying up-right embedded in sand, she is no-longer a thundering giant but a peaceful one hosting marine creatures instead of tons of cargo. She is a magnificent wreck dive site, one of the best in the Caribbean, covered in an incredible amount of colourful corals, she represents a successful artificial reef. The waters around the wreck are literally swarming with chromis, creole wrasse, several species of jacks and sergeant major fish.

After languishing in port for two years the Barbados Government decided to buy the SS Stavronikita with the intention of turning her into a dive site. On November 22nd 1978 explosive experts were hired to sink her. They positioned the ship with her bow facing the beach, at anchor in deep water off the coast and blew huge holes in the hull in several places.

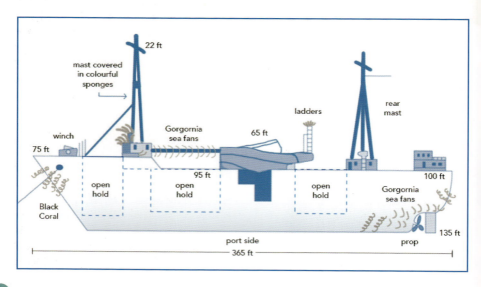

deep that bottom time is limited. A 30 - 40 minute dive here would be doing well.

The buoy is tied to the forward mast, which comes to within 25 ft of the surface. Most dive operators attach a reserve bottle to the rope in case a diver needs some extra air to finish their safety stop. The foremast structure resembles a long legged giant and is encrusted with a huge variety of colourful sponges and a forest of hydroids - among them branching, feather and slender varieties.

At one time divers could penetrate most areas of the wreck but in 2004 hurricane Ivan caused the bridge super structure to collapse and left the wreck damaged and unstable in many areas. This is a wreck that can only be dived if you have the required level of dive certification, nothing less than Advanced Padi certification or the equivalent. In many places it is far too dangerous even for highly trained technical wreck divers to enter. However, there is an area of the engine room that can be entered with reasonable safety but due to the depth and the fact that one is entering an overhead environment, the diver must be both Deep Diver and Wreck Diver qualified or be in training for those

The aim had been to land her upright on top of the reef with her mast out of the water to allow for snorkelling as well as scuba diving but she slid backwards and though upright landed in a sand channel between two reefs. Slightly deeper than planned but perfect depth for recreational scuba diving.

Lying at a depth of between 25 ft (the top of the mast) and 135 ft (at the keel) it will take several dives to see everything as the Stav - as she is affectionately known - is so big and so

Henrietta is framed by the fore mast corals.

specialties with a qualified instructor. There is plenty to explore without penetrating the wreck or going below 100 feet. Divers can take a guided tour which will take them down through the open cargo holds, passing from one to the next, through the holes in the bulkheads and also out through

Max and Emily take a moment to check their gauges.

to take full advantage of the prevailing current. The back mast is well worth the time to explore and though deeper, it is equally covered in an array of sponges, gorgonias and reef fish.

The Stavronikita is a dream for photographers especially when the visibility is good, it can be gin clear sometimes. Wide angle wreck shots are always a challenge but there is so

the blast holes in the hull. These holes in the hull let in valuable light that penetrates the interior. The holds have many deck levels, they present light areas to explore and a huge turtle is often found resting on a deck in the bow hold. Another route could be diving along the top deck from bow (75') to stern (100') and back, if current allows, just taking in the sheer size of the wreck.

The lower stern area is covered in encrusting sponges, gorgonian sea fans and black coral strands and the rudder and propeller are clearly visible. Above the mid-ship hold lies a horizontal beam covered in deep sea gorgonias, which have grown at a diagonal angle

The collapsed bridge area.

Just inside the midships on the starboard side.

If you need to get further certified in order to explore this wreck some more ask any of the dive centres, they can provide this service. This is a massive wreck and you won't find a more interesting one of this size in the Caribbean so don't miss it!

much colour on the wreck and fish life that the possibilities are endless. There are hand rails, ladders and all sorts of smaller structures that provide interesting lines and angles to make great photo opportunities.

For most divers the end of the dive is spent slowly ascending the huge forward mast which is one of the most colourful "reefs" you will see anywhere.

There are always plenty of fish on and around it and look in the yellow tube sponges for eels. Save time and air for this part as there is so much to see.

If the current is strong, which is can be at times, there is a long buoy line to hang on to for the duration of your safety stop.

Mika looks at an orange/yellow tube sponge on the fore mast.

The Cliff
BEACH CLUB
Derricks, St. James, Barbados

Lunch, Dinner, Nightlife
Open Tuesday - Sunday

reservations@thecliffbeachclub.com
1 (246) 432 0797

BELL BUOY   21

LOCATION: West Coast
DIVE TYPE: Drift • Reef
SKILL LEVEL: Minimum Novice

PHOTO TIP: Wide Angle
DEPTH: 30' - 100'
BUOY: Yes

The buoy is moored on the edge of a 50 ft wide sand channel and from here you can access two reefs; Horse Shoe reef and Bell Buoy. This whole reef area is roughly two football pitches wide and therefore you are recommended to always dive with a guide.

There are various ways to dive this and see different parts of the reef, but which ever way you decide to go, each direction can be a brilliant dive. For a deeper dive head south/west where the coral reef slopes down to 130ft + and a reef bridge actually connects it to Clarkes Bank.

The shallower dive features the widest variety of hard corals in one area on the island. The dive starts passing over some sand at 50 ft where you might find sting rays resting on the sand. The reef slowly builds up in growth with hard corals and some large sponge clusters. As you travel towards the left, sea plumes come into view and lots of blade fire coral. Large boulders of star coral are everywhere plus brain, elkhorn, staghorn, and pillar coral. Staghorn (see photo) and Elkhorn coral (see P47) are on the IUCN red list of critically endangered coral species and it is such a pleasure to see both corals on this dive, thriving and healthy.

There is a large old style anchor lying on the reef just before where there is an area of elkhorn coral. Elkhorn coral flourishes in shallow areas, it's rarely found deeper than 50ft because it needs strong sunlight. Its arms are thick and wide to survive wave action, however, anchors and divers are its enemy because it is very brittle.

Sea fans are scattered around and plenty of juvenile reef fish. Spotlight and striped parrotfish can be seen in numbers grooming the reef. Either way you dive at this site is excellent but because of its location, is susceptible to swells, currents and surges which can take visibility down to 40ft rather than 80ft and make the dive uncomfortable. Take the dive centers advice before you dive here.

Lucy hovers over an area of rare staghorn coral. By Henrietta Passos.

CLARKES BANK

LOCATION: West Coast
DIVE TYPE: Drift • Reef
SKILL LEVEL: Minimum Novice

PHOTO TIP: Wide Angle
DEPTH: 60' - 130'

This is a very large reef which runs perpendicular to the coastline and where the Atlantis Submarine visits. If you happen to be visiting the island with non-diving friends consider diving at the same time they are on the submarine. They will be able to see you through the large windows and you may be able to see them too. This is a super dive but seeing the submarine is a wonderful thrill in itself. The Atlantis is heard well before it is seen as the hum of her engines is amplified in the water. It is possible to get quite close and a photo of a fellow diver in the same frame as this majestic machine is possible, but whatever you do - do not touch it or go too close to it.

Because the Atlantis visits this reef no one is allowed to anchor or

Divers travel passed gorgonian fans.

A hawksbill turtle resting on the reef.

lay fishing lines or nets. Consequently, the entire reef area is in good health and full of life, although there is often a current running across it.

The dive route will vary depending on the current but would usually go along the reef further out and sometimes down the sloping reef edges. Bottom time is limited as this is a fairly deep dive.

Many varieties of hard and soft corals grow in abundance with red gorgonian fans standing out from the others, on top of the reef. Turtles are a common sight along with schools of horse-eye jacks. Once again, there is nowhere to set down on the reef as every inch is fought over by corals such as flower, brain and star. Some star coral colonies cover large areas in a single block and there are some huge yellow sponges reaching as high as five feet on this vast barrier reef.

95

CARLISLE BAY WRECKS   23

LOCATION: South/West Coast
DIVE TYPE: Wrecks• Return • Night
SKILL LEVEL: Minimum Novice

PHOTO TIP: All lenses
DEPTH: 20' - 60'
BUOY: Several inside the marine park

CARLISLE BAY MARINE PARK has an amazing 6 wrecks, all within a small area. This group of wrecks is unique among the Caribbean islands and another great incentive to dive here. It is possible, with the guidance of a good dive leader, to see all 6 wrecks on one dive. Four wrecks were sunk purposely, the most recent one the Bajan Queen in May 2002.

There is something for everyone on this dive site because each wreck is different from the other. Some are big and made of steel while others are small and made of cement or wood. Some have been down since 1919 while others are relative newcomers. They all attract their own distinct marine life, and all the wrecks host a variety of fish schools and brightly coloured encrusting sponges. Colonies of multi-coloured christmas tree worms and beautiful pink and lilac finger sponge are also common features.

This marine park is regularly used as an afternoon dive venue and for exciting night diving, probably the best night dive on the island. It is excellent for all aspects of photography but susceptible to swells, which can stir up the sand. The marine park is also easy to do as a beach dive. Just bring all your equipment down and park in the car park by the band stand in Carlisle Bay. You will be able to see several buoys inside the park which you can dive out to once you have taken a compass reading as you enter the water. There is also a conveniently located public tap to wash off afterwards in the car park.

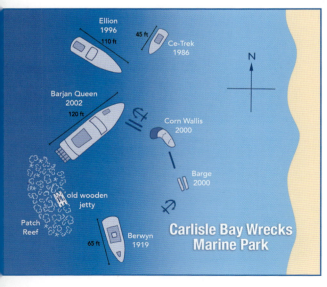
Carlisle Bay Wrecks Marine Park

Caesar Grunts hang out at the stern of the Berwyn.

The **BERWYN** has a canopy of sergeant major fish at various stages of development, they shower the first diver that goes near the wreck. Some dive companies do feed fish in the marine park, as they argue it draws the fish closer to the snorkelers that also visit. Because the fish come so close there is a good opportunity to get photos of some of the more shy reef fish such as squirrelfish, lizard fish, grunts and others.

The Berwyn, a 45 ft French tug boat, went down in 1919 and lies in only 25 feet of water. Considering her time spent underwater she is in a remarkable condition and by far the most encrusted wreck. The top deck area by the open hold is covered in flat sea anemones, there must be 100 of them!

It is possible to enter the open cargo area and peer through the side port holes, where a school of small mouthed grunts congregate; if approached slowly they often don't dart off. This is a good place to see eels, spotted moray, chain moray, and goldentail morays, but you will need to look low down in the wreck for them.

Sunk in May 2002 the **BAJAN QUEEN** is the largest wreck at 120 feet long. Lying in 40 ft of water she is so tall that she almost reaches the surface. The Bajan Queen started life as a tug boat around the 1960's and then later was converted into a 'party

These blackbar soldierfish hang out by the Bajan Queen stern.

One of the two huge propellers of the Bajan Queen

the bow.

Outside there are 2 huge propellers and this area usually has a school of blackbar soldier fish and yellow goat fish. The encrusting sponge colours are amazing. At night when the masses of cup coral polyps are out feeding the stern turns yellow.

boat'. She fell out of commission when bigger and better boats were launched on the party scene. But it is good to know that she has not out-grown her usefulness - as an artificial reef she will live forever. She was purposely sunk, the interior stripped, easy entry and exit has been facilitated.

Inside there is a large, easily accessible engine room which is inhabited by some banded coral shrimps. You can swim through this area and up passed a spiral staircase which will take you out to the top near

Yellow Frogfish.

A dark mantis shrimp in a sponge.

There is a small reef off the stern which is well worth a look, without much effort I found several anemones, cleaner shrimps and a seahorse.

Emily hovers over the Ce-Trek.

CE-TREK was an unwanted 45 foot cement boat left in the port to go to waste. In 1986 a couple of local divers decided to make a discarded boat into an artificial reef. This time they sunk the Ce-Trek near to another wreck and thus the idea of the Carlisle Bay Marine Park was born. The Ce-Trek has attracted plenty of marine life over the years and is well worth the extra swim. This wreck is now covered in colourful sponges where frogfish like to hangout. There is also a 'cleaning station' on the top part where fish can be seen hovering in the water whilst the tiny cleaner wrasse do their job.

The **ELLION**, a 110 foot freighter, was purposely sunk in 1996 and lies on a sand bed at 55 feet. There is a large open hold to explore and you easily go inside other areas that have plenty of natural light. Check out this wreck in the early morning, you might find a shy octopus. Around the wreck, you can sometimes find spadefish, barracuda, bar jacks, rainbow runners and garden eels.

The **CORNWALLIS** was a 60 ft Canadian freighter which sunk during the Second World War and re-located to this park in October 2000. Now, she is probably only 30 feet long and doesn't look like a boat at all. The left side is quite high, where small fish schools can hide and there is some nice sponge growth here. The right side is a large low arched part which is perfect for fish to use as a refuge; you will find lots of blackbar soldierfish and grunts congregating underneath here.

The **BARGE** was made of wood and has totally disintegrated into little more than only a couple of long pieces of wood; where someone has put an old telephone. Coral is growing on the wood and divers have found mantis shrimps in the sand at the northern end.

THE OLD FORT   24

LOCATION: South Coast
DIVE TYPE: Drift • Reef
SKILL LEVEL: Minimum Novice

PHOTO TIP: Macro & Close-up lenses
DEPTH: 35' - 70'
BUOY: Yes

This flat reef runs straight out from what remains of the historic old fort at the southern end of Carlisle Bay. The sandy seabed is scattered with coral boulders of varying sizes and small clusters of sponges. This is another good dive site for novice divers, as the shallow reef, at 35 feet, is well protected from currents and the reef harbours a variety of marine life.

Close inspection of the boulders can bring rewards, for under one boulder I found a local rarity - a lobster. You may also see the white spotted filefish. Although actually an orange colour, this fish is named for the white spots it shows when agitated or aggravated. This is a dive where you might see squid hovering above the reef, usually in numbers, not alone.

The reef fish population is plentiful with many glassyeye snappers, yellow goatfish, grunts, squirrelfish and blue chromis. A very pretty fish called a Highhat may be seen here. They look like the zebra of the underwater world, with black and white horizontal stripes along the length of the body. When juvenile this fish is recognised by an elegant long white dorsal fin that extends the entire length of its body. It flutters about low down in the reef hoping it won't be found.

Christmas tree worms decorate the small hard coral boulders, along with tiny goby fish. There are a number of sea anemones, some with resident cleaner shrimp.

Juvenile Highhat.

This squid is consuming a chromis fish, you can still see its tail. By Henrietta Passos.

CASTLE BANK   25

LOCATION: South Coast
DIVE TYPE: Drift • Reef
SKILL LEVEL: Minimum Novice

PHOTO TIP: Any lens
DEPTH: 50' - 120'
BUOY: Yes

If there is little or no current here, divers are led around the top of this banking/barrier reef, usually descending down on one side to about 80 feet or so. The dive continues up and along the top area at 60 feet. There is a drop-off, however, on both sides that leads to a depth of over 120 feet. The reef is in good condition and judging by the sea fans and gorgonia facing one way there is usually a generous current running across the reef - which makes this always a drift dive.

Once again the gentle swaying of the many sea plumes and rods adds tremendous softness to this reef. The ones I spotted harboured not only trumpetfish but also basket stars, which were curled up in the branches. Basket stars are a type of star-fish that have many long spidery arms. At night whilst anchored to something they unravel their arms to catch passing food particles, but during the day they are dormant.

Although short on giant barrel sponge this dive site does have a number of black and orange coloured crinoids, which are rare or absent in other areas. Crinoids are a member of the Echinoderm family, class feather stars. Feathery rays branch out 25 cms from a central disc. The arms curl gracefully toward their outer ends and bear tiny tentacular tube feet, which trap plankton from the water. It is usually found at moderate to deep locations on the reef, often attaching to the top of a coral promontory or sponge.

Trumpet fish are found on many dive sites.

Crinoids cling to a barrel sponge whilst they feed on passing plankton.

FRIARS CRAIG - RUM BARREL REEF - ASTA REEF

26

LOCATION: South Coast
DIVE TYPE: Wrecks • Return • Reefs
SKILL LEVEL: Minimum Novice
PHOTO TIP: All lenses
DEPTH: 20' - 60'
BUOY: Yes

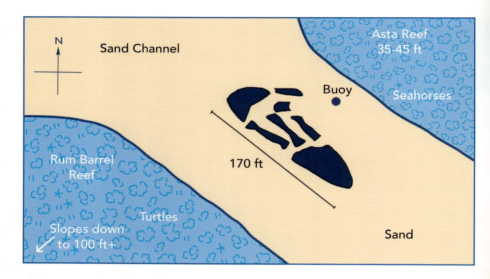

This is an excellent dive to suit all levels of divers from novice to expert and especially rewarding for photographers when the visibility is good. If the visibility is not great there are still numerous close up and macro subjects on the wreck and Asta reef.

The Friars Craig, a 170 foot freighter, was the sister ship to the Pamir but has not faired as well in her watery grave. Purposely sunk in 1985, she now lies at 50 feet on a large area of sand about 100 feet across in between two reefs. A serious storm, split her into three main unconnected segments, which means there are a number of different areas to explore. Lying on her port side she barely resembles a ship at all and it wasn't for her distinguishable bow, complete with part of a guard rail, she would just look like a mess of mangled metal.

Apart from the wreck there are two reefs to explore here. The deeper one Rum Barrel, is out towards the south/west and the shallower Asta reef is towards the shore. They are quite different and both worthy of exploring, but not on the same dive!

Calvin and Judy explore the bow section.

All segments of the wreck are covered in various corals and there are plenty of photographic opportunities. There are gorgonias, sea fans and various sponges on all sections. Adding to the delightful array of flora are innumerable reef fish, the most notable are yellow grunts, sergeant major, blue tang, trumpetfish, yellow goatfish and chromis.

A giant mantis shrimp, very rare, has also been seen around the bow section (see photo) however, like most marine creatures they don't stay in the same place for very long.

Wrecks like this one, set in secluded calm and sandy areas, are an ideal retreat for rays, turtles and octopus. If you get the chance to visit the wreck in a small group it would be well worth staying here rather than moving off to the reef. There is a large variety of marine life with good photographic opportunities in easy conditions. Many dive centres talk about a large resident hawksbill turtle. He is regularly found

A giant mantis shrimp at the top of its' hole.

105

Friars Craig stern section.

sponge in this area where frogfish are often found.

When you have seen enough of the wreck you can move across the sand, past the buoy line to **Asta reef** which gives the impression of a reef in infancy. Most of the coral growth is in miniature, except for some large odd-shaped barrel sponges. In fact they look rather like folded-up pizzas standing up-right. Among the fronds of the soft corals on Asta reef, you can also find seahorses, flamingo tongue snails and younger turtles.

A flamingo tongue snail moving across a sea fan.

resting on the sand in the mid-ship area snuggled under an overhang.

The stern section is pretty well intact, grunts inhabit a part of the interior and there is some lovely yellow

A school of small mouth grunts huddle in the stern section.

This is a small section of what is a very large reef. Asta reef runs all along the Hastings shoreline and one can almost say it's a continuation of the Pieces Of Eight reef. Features include tall sea plumes and because it's shallow there is plenty of light for strobe free photography.

Alternatively, you can choose to dive **Rum Barrel** reef which is in the opposite direction across a 60 ft wide sand channel. This is a wide reef which if you keep going will descend down to over 100 feet. This reef is well worth a visit with large sponges, hard and soft corals and a chance to see turtles, rays and … well who knows what might swim by!

Asta reef.

BARBADOS DIVE GUIDE

DIVE SITES

Friars Craig - Rum Barrel Reef - Asta Reef

COURTESY RENT A CAR
Reservations - (246) 431- 4160
Fax (246) 429-6387
E: reservations@courtesyrentacar.com
W: www.courtesyrentacar.com

COURTESY RENT A CAR has been providing car rental services in Barbados since the mid 1970's. By providing quality vehicles at competitive rates with reliable friendly service, Courtesy has become the most recognizable name in car rentals.

We operate four conveniently located offices at The Grantley Adams International Airport, WIldey St. Michael, Charnocks Christ Church and The Bridgetown Cruise Terminal. If clients prefer, vehicles can be delivered to their hotel or residence, during regular working hours at no additional charge.

We offer Nissan, Hyundai and Fiat vehicles for rental in all popular ranges from Economy cars to Luxury SUV's.

Courtesy has recently introduced the Courtesy Customer rewards card, a value added package of savings at local restaurants and attractions. Enjoy a self driven tour of our island and visit the amazing Harrison's Cave, the Animal Flower Cave or for the more adventurous a tour of the islands' many stunning beaches, all at your own pace.

CARLEYNE   27

LOCATION: South Coast
DIVE TYPE: Drift • Reef
SKILL LEVEL: Minimum Novice

PHOTO TIP: Wide Angle
DEPTH: 60' - 90'
BUOY: Yes

There is no mooring line on this outer dive site where the reef, at its shallowest at only 60 feet means quite a short dive compared to other sites. So if you are diving here I recommend you dive along the outer reef edge (within your certification level) which slopes down over 120ft plus, you never know what might be cruising passed.

The dive guide will take you on a tour of the upper part of this pretty reef along to the far southern end where the reef has an extension off to the right. The reef is over 100ft long and 60ft wide in most places and is fairly flat.

There are no distinct reef features but there are lots of hard and soft corals which totally cover the top. Large barrel sponges, gorgonias and a few sea whips stand out, along with bright orange elephant ear and yellow sponges. The reef is short on fish life but you will see some common reef fish and perhaps a green moray eel.

There are a few yellow tube sponge clusters and one dive I was lucky enough to find a spotted eel looking for food inside it. Various varieties of gobies and shrimps live inside these big sponges feeding on plankton that ends up in the tube, so take a look inside them when you see them on a reef. I have also found many frogfish inhabiting areas around sponges over the years, they seem to blend in with them very well.

A spotted moray eel searches for food inside yellow tube sponges.

A diver passes by a large yellow tube sponge cluster. By Paul Colley.

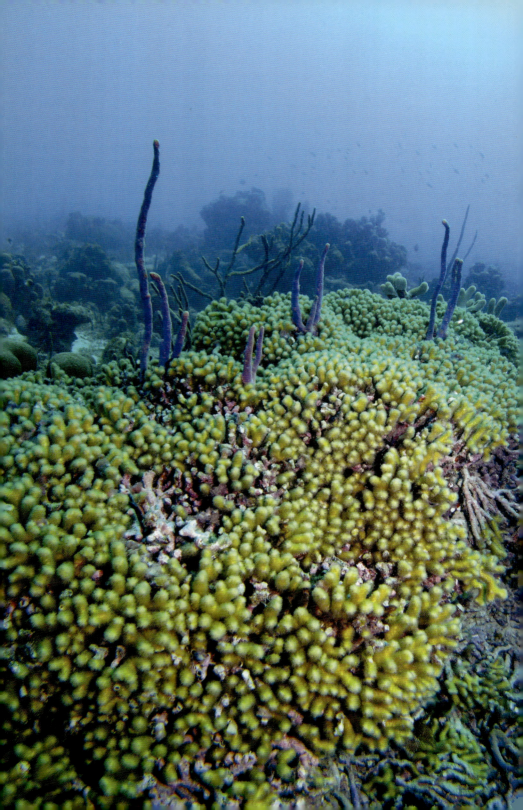

PIECES OF EIGHT

28

LOCATION: South Coast
DIVE TYPE: Drift • Reef
SKILL LEVEL: Novice

PHOTO TIP: Any Lens
DEPTH: 25' - 75'

Most dive companies on the south coast use this shallow reef as a second dive or afternoon dive, it's a lovely easy dive with an active varied reef. The mooring buoy is anchored at 25 feet on a flat reef, which consists of small hard coral boulders interspersed with sandy areas. The coral is mostly brain coral and many have clusters of christmas tree worms growing on them.

From the buoy line the dive continues along the edge of the reef at 60 ft, which gently slopes down to 100 ft on one side. Many reef fish inhabit the small overhanging coral ridges, including peacock flounders with cleaner shrimps cleaning the tiny parasites from their bodies. Other fish action may include a school of sennet and blue tangs.

After a short distance along the reef stunning mountains of finger coral colonies at least 30' wide by 50'-70' in length, create massive ridges running down the reef. In amongst the hundreds of coral fingers are tiny reef fish, shrimps and crabs that use the coral as a hiding place. On close inspection the small coral fingers are covered in tiny polyps, which during the day may be extended, giving them a fuzzy velvety appearance. This would make a good night dive on a calm evening.

Close up of yellow pencil coral polyps.

Mountains of yellow pencil coral colonies are along this dive site. By Henrietta Passos.

**PARADISE SURF SCHOOL
with Bruce Mackie**

P: + 246 826 8999
E: paradisesurf@hotmail.com

SURF LESSONS:

Professional surfer Bruce Mackie and his team specialise in teaching first timers and beginners to surf in a fun and safe environment.

We ensure that beginner lessons are conducted in small gentle waves and we are the only surf school on the island that keeps groups small.

We promise that for every one instructor there will only be a maximum of 4 students giving you the one on one time you need so you can ride the waves super quickly. **Duration 2 hours.**

STAND UP PADDLE LESSON & TURTLE TOURS:

Our Stand Up Paddle Turtle Tour is fun for the whole family and really easy!

We start you off with a short beach instruction, showing everyone how to use our brand new top of the line equipment.

The tour includes paddling in Carlisle Bay over calm beautiful blue waters to the ship wrecks where we stop to feed the fish and snorkel, from there we paddle over to our second stop where guests can meet and greet the turtles.

This breathtaking marine experience is topped off with refreshments on the beach. **The tour is for 90 minutes.**

Fun for the whole family!

For these activities guests should bring a towel, sunscreen, sport appropriate swimwear and cash for payment.

CARIBBEE

LOCATION: South Coast
DIVE TYPE: Drift • Reef
SKILL LEVEL: Minimum Novice

PHOTO TIP: Wide Angle
DEPTH: 60' - 90'
BUOY: Yes

This dive goes in a westerly direction along the south coast barrier reef. The reef is dome shaped with drop-offs on either side going down to 150 feet. It is recommended to stay on top of the reef at approximately 60 feet, allowing a maximum no decompression dive time at that depth of 40 minutes.

The top of the reef is about 80 feet across and is covered in huge deep red gorgonias, purple sea fans and sea rods. They are all so perfectly spaced along the reef that it looks like they have somehow been planted. They are undoubtedly the main attraction of this dive.

There is the usual sprinkling of fish, but not as many as seen on other dives. During the months of March - April something on the reef maybe spawning, and great clouds of tiny eggs envelop the reef in a white haze. This is quite a rare sight, but it's beautiful to witness nature in action. As with other areas along the south coast sponge growth is less profound but equally pretty.

Because the reef drops away deeply on both sides it is advisable to watch the edges of the reef for passing marine life. Barracuda, turtles, eagle rays & pelagic fish are all noted visitors.

Beautiful gorgonian fans.

THE BOOT   30

LOCATION: South Coast
DIVE TYPE: Drift • Reef
SKILL LEVEL: Minimum Novice

PHOTO TIP: Wide Angle
DEPTH: 30' - 90'
BUOY: Yes

This is a wonderful turtle dive in Barbados, with sightings of green and hawksbill turtles almost guaranteed. In fact, close encounters with these beautiful, peaceful creatures are a regular aspect of this dive. The dive gets its name because it's roughly shaped like a boot, who am I to question that?

Descending the buoy line will lead you down to a 30 ft deep sandy area on the edge of a flat reef which is covered in soft sea plumes and sea fans. These soft gently swaying corals invite you across the reef and bestow a feeling of relaxation.

Given an ample supply of their favourite variety of sponge, it is no wonder so many turtles are attracted to this reef. The Boot is a natural safe haven with perfect camouflage and a steady food supply. The turtles vary in size from juvenile to large adult males, some of which even have remoras attached to them. Turtles can stay underwater for up to 1 ½ hours before having to surface for air, and usually choose soft places to rest, such as where there are large areas of sponge growth. When they are lying still they are very hard to see until you are almost on top of them. They usually see you first and move. This is a good photo opportunity as they take time to get themselves up off the reef because of their cumbersome, heavy shells.

The reef top is about 30 ft across and the outer edge slopes down at a 35 degree angle to a flat sandy area at 90 ft, where sting rays can be found. Naturally, here as with many other sites, the soft arms of the sea plumes are used by trumpet fish for concealment.

The dive generally goes across the reef towards the outer slope and along to the far end towards the right, then turns back up along the inside where there are large pieces of an old boat lying on the sand. Here the sloping reef side is quite steep but levels out as it comes up to join the shallow inner reef edge. There is no need to go back to the boat, divers are picked up where they surface.

A green turtle rests in between the corals.

THE MUFF   31

LOCATION: South Coast
DIVE TYPE: Drift • Reef
SKILL LEVEL: Experienced Open Water Diver

PHOTO TIP: Wide Angle
DEPTH: 70' - 100'
BUOY: Yes

The mooring line on this dive is located at a depth of 70 feet at the top of this long ridge-like reef. The top is about 80 feet across and drops off sharply on the seaward side to more than 150 feet, while the other side slopes to a depth of 100 feet. To prolong the length of the dive time it is best to stay on top of the reef rather than venture down the sides. In any case there is a wealth of marine life on the top.

Largely because this is an outer/deeper reef there is an abundance of huge sea fans, sea plumes and whips where strong currents prevail, providing valuable food. As on many Barbados reefs, large barrel sponges break up this undulating reef, don't swim past, but check inside for banded coral shrimps, fish and crabs. The growth of large cascading brown lumpy finger sponge is prolific here and orange elephant ear sponges add a splash of bright colour.

The large and small brain coral boulders are frequented by lizardfish in particular and blackbar soldier fish can often be found hiding beneath soft corals. The usual sprinkling of reef fish scurry about the reef but not in prolific numbers. You will most likely see schools of boga fish on this dive, above the reef or when they sometimes come down to the reef in a long stream.

Turtles and barracudas can be seen cruising the reef looking for food. If you see a barracuda don't worry. They are not the vicious fish some people make them out to be. Like most 'animals' they are curious about us divers and may approach for that reason. But ultimately they are highly sought after by local spear-fisherman and so after a quick look usually disappear off asap!

Lookout for this orange/yellow sponge on the reef.

ST. LAWRENCE REEF

32

LOCATION: South Coast
DIVE TYPE: Drift • Reef
SKILL LEVEL: Minimum Novice

PHOTO TIP: Macro & Close-up lenses
DEPTH: 30' - 50'

There is no buoy to pin point the start of this dive but you can descend anywhere along this fringing reef. The dive is usually led towards the west with the reef on your right shoulder. Unfortunately, visibility on this dive can be hindered if the wind is high or if it has just rained.

The top of the reef is at 25 feet and gently slopes down to 45 feet where it meets a bed of sand. I would encourage you to look for sting rays and conch shells on the sand in this area. The sand slopes away over a ridge further out to greater depths. This would also be a good opportunity to get photos of garden eels because the flat sand bed is shallow and expansive.

The dive guide will take you along the reef's edge where you should look out for turtles, barracuda, octopus and anemones to name the less ordinary subjects. Nooks and crannies under rock boulders and soft swaying sea plume arms may harbour fish and eels, so this is not a dive to be rushed.

After waiting a few minutes this conch slowly came out of its shell.

CLOSE ENCOUNTER/ DOVER

33

LOCATION: South Coast
DIVE TYPE: Drift • Reef
SKILL LEVEL: Minimum Novice

PHOTO TIP: Close-up & Macro
DEPTH: 30' - 45'

This dive site has been given two names so which one is used will depend on which dive centre you are diving with. Located on the shallow fringing reef that runs parallel to the south coast, this dive is just off Dover Beach, hence its second name.

The reef at 30 feet is usually visible from the surface, and following a free descent the dive is led in a westerly direction, keeping the reef on the right shoulder. Diving along the edge, the reef meets the sand at a depth of 45 feet, and here you may encounter turtles and sting rays. The reef edge sweeps in and then out again, so diving in a reasonable straight line will necessitate some travel over sand.

The sand area, however, has quite a few small groups of tiny feather dusters, razorfish and some garden eels. Garden eels are very shy and usually withdraw into their tiny holes whenever something comes near. They are of course worried about predators. Approached very slowly and low down to the sand, they sometimes come back out and will pose quite nicely for the camera. This may take some time though, so watch out that you don't lose the rest of the dive group.

The reef is covered with sea fans and soft gorgonias interspersed with hard corals, rock and small colourful sponges. The bright yellow stripes of smallmouth and French grunts add colour to the reef scene as they shimmer past. Like squirrelfish, they are not loner fish, but instead prefer the safety-in-numbers principle. Trumpet fish and goldentail eels are also common.

Although this reef is close to the shore a few pelagic fish such as bar jacks and cero pass by, and colourful chromis feed on the plankton above the reef.

For divers or photographers looking for the smaller reef creatures there are a number of purple tipped anemones.

A yellow feather duster or 'tube worm', taken during the day, using a high f-stop and very fast shutter speed. (f8, 1/2000)

HIGH WIRE

LOCATION: South Coast
DIVE TYPE: Drift • Reef
SKILL LEVEL: Experienced Open Water Diver

PHOTO TIP: Any Lens
DEPTH: 60' - 100'

High Wire is one of the furthest sites along the South coast, near to Oistins Bay, and therefore not always a pleasant journey when the wind is up or the sea is rough. For divers, however, it is well worth the effort.

The buoy is moored in 60 feet on top of a beautiful healthy reef that is covered in hard and soft corals. This outer dive site is usually blessed with good visibility because it lies quite a way off shore where currents remove run-off water and provide rich nourishment for the corals. Rather like some of the more northerly dives of the west coast, this reef is very easy on the eye. It is full of colour and marine life and there is a sense of peacefulness here.

The dive can go either to the west or east depending on currents or preferences. It is regarded as a deep first dive because the reef slopes away, quite steeply on one side, to beyond 100 feet. As this is an outer banking reef dive it is best to keep one eye looking out to sea in case something large and interesting goes by. The site gets its name from a large wire cable which has been abandoned and is now part of the reef.

There is an abundance of large brown sponge clusters along with other coloured sponges. The hard coral formations are principally plate, star and brain. These are complemented by the presence of deep sea fans, sea plumes and sea whips. Some of the lower slopes have huge black coral strands spiralling out like giant cork screws.

The fish life complements the reef and, other than the usual common varieties, the addition of queen angel fish adds brilliance as they dart around. Queen angelfish are very skittish and I would warn against being drawn deeper down to get a closer look.

The upper water area is teaming with boga fish, a small blue/silver fish shaped like a long sausage. Mackerels, jacks and yellow snapper can also be seen passing by.

Lavender finger sponge stands out on this sloping reef.

MOUNT CHARLIE 35

LOCATION: South Coast
DIVE TYPE: Drift • Reef
SKILL LEVEL: Experienced Open Water diver.

PHOTO TIP: Wide Angle & Mid Lens
DEPTH: 60' - 100'
BUOY: Yes

Mount Charlie is an extension of the south banking reef and it protrudes out at right angles to the main reef. There is a steep slope on the right or east side while the other side slopes more gently. The top of the reef where the mooring rope is attached lies at 60 feet, close to some large hard coral formations. One of them has a cleaning station serviced by a dozen or so bluehead wrasse. This wrasse is a small fish, the adult having a bright blue head and green body while the juvenile version is completely bright yellow.

Mackerel scad is a fish that schools in numbers and they can be seen rushing about above the reef. They don't feed on the reef and only come down to use cleaning stations, such as the one previously mentioned.

The reef is a garden of hard and soft corals. Look closely among them and it is possible to find large spiny spider crabs, lizardfish, pufferfish, peacock flounders and many other creatures. The common reef fish are present in good supply, but nothing prolific. There is more brown sponge growth than other kinds, and as such one could say this dive lacks colour.

Scads, a type of mackerel can be seen schooling on this deep reef.

THE FINGER   36

LOCATION: South Coast
DIVE TYPE: Drift • Reef
SKILL LEVEL: Minimum Novice

PHOTO TIP: Any Lens
DEPTH: 30' - 80'

The site is opposite the Welcome Inn Hotel on the south coast and, as the name suggests, is a finger-shaped reef projecting out from the fringing reef. There is no buoy so a free descent to the top of the reef at 30 feet is necessary, which on most days is observable.

The finger, though only moderately covered in a mixture of hard corals, sea whips, sea plumes and purple sea fans, does give the impression it has been planned by a garden designer. Each kind of sponge adds its own colourful accent and dimension to the reef. With plenty of reef fish such as peacock flounders, damselfish, squirrelfish, yellow and red snapper, grunts and rock beauties, the overall appearance is more than satisfying.

It is usual to begin the dive on the left side, traveling all the way around to the other side. On the left side the reef slopes sharply down to a sandy bottom at 100 feet, and this is the best place to do the deepest part of the dive. There have been sightings of octopus and juvenile hawksbill turtles along here at a depth of 75 feet.

Schools of blue and brown chromis dance above the reef, energetically feeding on passing plankton.

Where the point flattens out and joins the main reef bank the photographic subjects are plentiful. Here in 30 ft there is plenty of time, air permitting, to look for specific marine animals like Highhat fish, pufferfish, scorpionfish, eels and goatfish.

Sting Ray.

This is a rare reverse colour goldentail moray eel. By Henrietta Passos.

GRAEME HALL SHALLOWS

37

LOCATION: South Coast
DIVE TYPE: Drift • Reef
SKILL LEVEL: Novice

PHOTO TIP: Any Lens
DEPTH: 50' - 90'

This barrier reef is about 400 feet long and 40 feet in width and is not attached to any other reef. Situated a long way down the south coast, near Oistins Bay, this reef is well known by local fishermen. There is some red algae growth on this reef and when it has just rained visibility is very poor because it is near the shore.

The top of the reef starts at 50 feet and gradually deepens to 70 feet as you travel west. Both sides slope down to flat sand at a depth of 90 feet. It is advisable not to go too deep for too long at the beginning of the dive or you may end up with a shortened dive.

Once again the reef is covered in soft corals with some large flowing sea plumes and whips that particularly stand out. Trumpet fish thrive along with parrotfish, scrawled filefish, peacock flounders, butterfly fish, trunk fish and other common varieties. Turtles and barracuda are attracted to the area, perhaps because of the ample camouflage of barrel sponges and sea fans.

Sea fans are found on many of the dive sites.

Large barrel sponges stand erect on the reef slope.

THE STUDY

38

LOCATION: East Coast, Consett Bay
DIVE TYPE: Drift • Reef
SKILL LEVEL: Advanced Experienced

PHOTO TIP: Wide Angle
DEPTH: 25' - 120'
* Challenging Diving

This is a long reef which runs parallel to the shore just north of Consett Bay and like nothing you see on the south or west coast dives. The reef should really be described as bedrock and is sparsely covered with hard and soft corals and some sea fans. But what makes this dive worth the effort is the seascape, where massive rock formations and boulders create swim-throughs and tunnels which harbour all sorts of creatures. Nurse sharks are often found resting in the various caves and underwater ledges along this dive.

Southern rays which are bigger than sting rays can be found more often over here and turtles are regularly seen. But it is the only place you might and that's a big might, see leatherback turtles, because they lay their eggs on the east coast beaches during the spring season.

Visibility is hit and miss, a miss can mean a very poor dive, but at least the boat ride is shorter than other sites.

Southern Sting Ray. By Henrietta Passos.

Tunnels and swim-throughs are features of this dive. By Henrietta Passos.

RAGGED POINT 39

LOCATION: East Coast, Consett Bay
DIVE TYPE: Drift • Reef
SKILL LEVEL: Advanced Experienced

PHOTO TIP: Wide Angle
DEPTH: 25' - 90'
* Challenging Diving

The top of this small reef starts at about 25ft and runs parallel to the shore. It is best to go over the edge of the shelf as soon as you can to get away from the swell and strong currents. The top of the reef is sparsely covered with sea fans and other corals that can survive in a strong surge and brutal wave actions.

The reef is in excellent condition, literally teaming with fish and it steeply slopes down to a sandy bottom at 90 ft. Schools of barracuda, chub and grunts swim around so thick they are like a wall in front of you. Large rays and nurse sharks can also be seen.

The current can be deceptively strong at times and if you come up on to the top of the reef it can be impossible to swim back over the edge of the shelf again.

A big school of smallmouth grunts inhabit the reef wall. By Henrietta Passos.

Schools of chub are common on this dive site. By Henrietta Passos.

ADDITIONAL DIVE SITES

There are a number of good dives that either don't merit a full write up or it is not the right time to include them in this edition. I want to give you a feel for these additional dive sites, in case you wish to explore any of them with one of the dive centers.

BRIANNA H WRECK
60' - 130' • Carlisle Bay

The Brianna went down as a ship wreck and not purposely sunk, very recently in 2014 which means she has not been cleared for diving. One day she will be a super wreck dive once she has been made safe for divers. She sits on a sandy bed upright but with little surrounding reef.

THE CHASM
West Coast near Maycocks

This is a very difficult dive site to plan because more often than not sea swells churn up the water and make the underwater visibility less than 20ft and the waves make it impossible to approach. But when calm, you can see big schools of various fish milling around rock walls and large boulders over a sandy bottom.

LIGHTHOUSE DROP-OFF
Below the Chasm

This was a nice reef dive with plenty to see but recently the reef has deteriorated so much it is not worthy of a full page. A sloping reef wall dive with various hard corals and you can see squid and living conch shells on the sand.

G SPOT
South Coast

So named by G the dive guide. (his favourite dive)

This dive is called a few different names, can be dived several ways and it can be done as a beach dive. Two lovely reefs are separated by a deep sand channel. There is every chance you will see an eagle ray and Elkhorn coral grows in the very shallow area off the beach. This dive is a long boat ride down to near Oistins. I need to dive here to give you a full account and it will certainly be included next time.

The top of the reef around Ragged Point. By Henrietta Passos.

A peppermint goby sits on valley brain c[oral]

Blakey's
on the boardwalk
Bar & Restaurant

Hastings, Chistchurch
T: 228-5284
E: blakeysbar@gmail.com
Open for lunch and dinner
Tues - Sat from 11:30am
Reservations and take-away

Blakey's is an informal restaurant on the sea front in Hastings on the south coast which serves great pizza, curries, local dishes and daily specials.

Inside, the bar has a great select[ion] of cocktails and wine and seve[ral] TV's provide various sports chann[els] from around the world.

There is lively entertainment with [a] variety of live music and DJ's th[at] play throughout the week.

Good Food Good Lime Good Mu[sic]

tripadvis[or]

A FEW WORDS ABOUT HOW BARBADOS IS WORKING TO ...
PROTECT THE CORAL REEFS
...AND ECOSYSTEMS THAT SURROUND THE ISLAND.

Barbados is fortunate in having a government that recognises the value of its coral reefs for coastal protection, production of white sand, supporting biodiversity, dive tourism, aesthetic beauty, food security and livelihood support.

To manage such a valuable resource, with various stressors requires the collaboration of multiple 'players'. Barbados is among the leaders in the Caribbean in adopting a 'holistic and integrated' approach and has a dedicated Coastal Zone Management Unit (CZMU). The unit is also responsible for public education on coastal matters, for monitoring the health of the island's coral reefs, water quality, coastal currents, wave energy and placement and maintenance of mooring buoys. CZMU also conducts research to inform policy and management action.

The CZMU has benefitted from the considerable body of marine research undertaken by two research institutions on the island – the Bellairs Research Institute and the University of the West Indies and continue to receive expert guidance and engage in significant collaborative research with the latter. Over the last few decades they have attracted international funding support and instigated many important coastal protection projects.

A major ongoing initiative, the Coastal Risk Assessment and Management Programme, which has a significant element focussed on reef preservation and rehabilitation, is ensuring that Barbados is well placed to face ongoing and future threats to its coastal resources. This programme will help to prepare the way for comprehensive marine spatial planning by creating a detailed island-wide marine habitat map, assessing water pollution sources and investigating the feasibility of a coral nursery and mapping endangered corals.

Foureye butterfly fish flutter across a reef.

Despite these efforts marine management is a complex process and locals, visitors and divers can all help by playing their part. For instance if you are a visitor you can chose to stay in a "green hotel", which means they operate several environment friendly processes such as; recycling, effective waste treatment, solar power, reduced water and towel use. Likewise if you are a resident you can introduce the same effective measures into your daily routines; check out the Be The Change Barbados website for helpful advice.

www.bethechangebarbados.org

A bicolour damselfish hove[rs] above a rare amber penshe[ll]. By Lucy Aga[ce]

BARBADOS UNDERWATER PHOTOGRAPHY ACADEMY

W: www.scubachannels.com/bupa
E: lucy@scubachannels.com
T: 230 5464

The Barbados Underwater Photographic Academy is owned and run by Lucy Agace, who has 29 years of experience diving all over the world in 42 different countries.

Lucy spends over half the year on Barbados and is available for private and group underwater photography lessons. She is a qualified INON underwater photography instructor, loves teaching and has been successfully doing so for many years.

The INON level 1 course combined with her experience brings the expertise needed to guarantee that anyone from beginners upwards will learn how to take quality images, improve strike rates and master simple but effective techniques.

Lucy believes it's important to understand marine life behaviour in order to photograph it well. If you can't find, see, know where to look for or how to approach your subjects then you won't get to first base - says Lucy. Having dived here for over 16 years she knows the best spots for stunning seascapes and is a great guide when it comes to finding a variety of creatures such as - seahorses, mantis shrimps and frogfish.

Affordable scuba diving photographic holiday packages can be organised for you, details for this are on the webpage above or simply contact Lucy direct.

Lucy prefers to use a compact camera system where you can change lenses underwater and vary the subject choice during a dive and compact cameras are much lighter than dslr cameras and therefore easier to handle. If required Olympus XZ 2 cameras are available for rent and there are various lenses and strobes for students to try out during the course.

ENDORSEMENT:
I could tell immediately that Lucy was passionate about her work. She was able to impart her depth of knowledge to my particular photographic needs. Lucy was an excellent motivator, personable and artistically inspiring. Myles 2014

A long snout seahorse.

SEAHORSES

Everyone loves seahorses, like dolphins we are drawn to them and seem to get an enormous amount of pleasure from seeing one - in the flesh and preferably in its' natural environment, not an aquarium. They are probably the cutest marine animal you will ever see and also one of the most vulnerable.

Barbados is very fortunate in that it seems provide the natural habitat for seahorses to flourish. There are two species of seahorses found here the Lined and Longsnout Seahorse, both are generally found low down on the reef with their tails wrapped around pieces of sponge or other grounded corals. They vary in colour from dark brown - reddish brown - orange - yellow.

What do we know about them - well we know that the male of the species incubates the eggs but how do they get there? He's male right?

Firstly many seahorse species mate for life and perform daily courtship rituals that include changing colour. The female inserts her eggs through an oviduct into the male's pouch. The male attaches onto a

A yellow lined seahorse looks right into my camera lens. Lucy Agace

A lined seahorse.

nearby coral for the gestation period of several weeks. He gives birth by contractions and the miniature young seahorses squirt out of his pouch over several minutes or hours. Once out they have to fend for themselves.

They are classified as fish, easy to approach and rarely swim off - but they are surprisingly agile swimmers when they do!

Never touch a seahorse because you might damage their tiny fins which they use to move.

They feed on passing plankton and small fish and can change colour to blend into their surroundings making them very hard to find.

They have few predators because they are so boney and indigestible. Humans are their only real predator!

Please don't buy a dead or alive seahorse or any derivative of it all you are doing is providing the sales market.

Seahorses can be found on many of the shallower reefs around Barbados but you are more likely to see them on these dive sites: 3, 5, 11, 19, 23, 26.

INDEX

Bold numbers denote a photograph.

A. Angelfish, 75
    French, 53, **57**
    Queen, 121
Anemone, **59**, 79, 97, 98, 101, 119, 121
Atlantic Spade Fish, 23, 61, 67
Atlantic Squid, 17, 70, **100**, 135
Atlantis Submarine, 14, 15, 94

B. Balloonfish, **73**
Bajan Queen Wreck, 97, **98**
Barbados Blue Water Sports, 36-38
Barge, The 99
Barracuda, 19, 21, 53, 55, 77, 99, 113, 117
Basket Starfish, **22**, 103
Batfish, Bottlenose, **21**, **53**
BDOA - Barbados Dive Operators Assoc, 29
Berwyn, The 23, 97
Black Durgon, 47
Blackbar Soldier Fish, 57, 61, 81, **84**, **97**, 99, 117
Blenny, Sailfin, **20**, 52
    Pike, **20**, 52
Blue Tang, 17, 83, 105, 111
Boga, 23, 65, 77, 117, 123
Burrfish, 70
Butterfly Fish, Foureye, **74**, 83, 129
BSTP, Barbados Sea Turtle Project, 19

C. Carlisle Bay, 13, **23**, 96, 101
Carlisle Bay Marine Park Wrecks, 13, 23, **96**, 99
Cement Plant Pier, 20, 50-53
Cero, 23, 121
Ce-Trek, Wreck **99**
Chamber Hyperbaric, **25**, 25
Christmas Tree Worms, 83, 85, 101, 111,
Chromis, 13, 17, 23, 49, 53, 65, 79, 101, 127
Chub, 13, 47, **132**
Clam, **138**
Cleaning Station, 65, 99, 125
Climate, 10
Conch, **119**, 135
Coral, Black, 56, **57**, 61, 89, 123
    Brain, 22, 49, 85, 93, 95, 111, 123
    Branching, 18
    Elkhorn, **47**, 93, 135
    Encrusting Fire Coral, **18**, **90**, **92**, 93
    Finger, 18, 71, **100**, **111**
    Pillar, 21, **78**, 93
    Plate Star, 22, 49, **60**, 93, 123
    Plate Fire, 93
    Staghorn, **92**, 93
    Star, 22, 71, 85, 95, 123
    Yellow Cup, **53**, 98
Cornwallis, The 99
Crabs, 111
    Arrow, **79**, 81
    Coral, 17, 27, 70, **71**
    Spider, 81, 117, 125
    Flame Box, **21**
Crinoid, 22, **24**, **102**, 103

D. Damselfish, 13, 75, **92**, 127, **138**
Dive Centres, 28-29
Dive Site List & Map, 44-45
Diving Overview, 16-24

E. Eels, 19, 33, 53, 67, 69, 71, 73, 119, 127
    Chain, 97

  Garden, 17, 58, 99, 119, 121
  Goldentail, 97, 121, **126**
  Green Moray, **76**
  Sharptail, 53
  Spotted, 53, 61, 70, **72**, 79, 97, **109**
  Snake, 79
Ellion Wreck, 99
Essential Information, 11

F. Fan, Sea, **17**, 18, 19, **20**, 56, **57**, 67, 77, 78, 93, 105, 115, **129**
  Purple, 61, **106**, 113, 127, **134**
Feather Duster, 79, 85, **120**, 121
Filefish,
  Whitespotted, 51, 55, 73, 101
  Scrawled, 53, 61, 63, 73, 75, 129
  Slender, **21**
Fire Worm, **59**
Flamingo Tongue Snail, 17, **106**
Flying Gurnard, 53, **58**
Folkstone Marine Park, 13, 45
Friars Craig, Wreck 23, 104, **105**
Frogfish, 17, **20**, 52, **52**, 70, **98**, 99, 106, 109,

G. Geology, 10
Gorgonia, 19, 22, **48**, 61, 77, 78, 89, **90**, **94**, 106, **113**
Goby, Cleaning **72**, **76**
  Peppermint, **136**
Grunts, 57, 73, 83, **97**, 99, 101, 105, 121, 127

H. Harrison's Cave, 10
Hazell's Water World, 8
Highhat, **101**, 127
Hightide, 32-33
History, 7
Hogfish, Spanish 49, 55, 65, 79, 85
Hydroids, 87, **88**

J. Jacks, 17, 51, **58**, 77, 95, 99, 121, 123
Jawfish, **20**, 53, **70**
Junior PADI, 28

L. Lettuce Leaf Slug, 13
Lionfish, **9**, 49
Lizardfish, 55, 61, 69, 30, 97, 117, 125
Lobster, 101
  Slipper, 59

M. Mackerels, 17, 23, 58, 77, 123, **124**

N. Night Diving, 24, 96

O. Oceansports Technical Diving, 39, **39**
Octopus, **24**, 33, **50**, 59, 99

P. Pamir, The 23, **56**-59
Parrotfish, 13, **24**, 55, 63, 65, 75, 79, **81**, 83, 93, 129
Peacock Flounder, **21**, 53, **75** 80, 111, 125, 127
Pencil Star, 13
Pipefish, 53, 83
Plumes, Sea 16, 19, 61, **68**, **74**, 77, 85, 93, **107**, 115, 129
Pufferfish, 53, 70, 125, 127

R. Rainbow Runners, 17, 23, 99
Rays, 15, 107
  Eagle, 16, 17, 19, 70, 79, 113
  Manta, 18
  Sting, 18, 71, 93, 115, 119, 121, **127**
  Southern Sting, **127**, 131
Recreation, 12
Reefers & Wreckers, 30-31, 47
Rock Beauty, 49, 55, 127
Rogers Scuba Shack, 34-35

S. Safari Boat, 13,
Sand Diver, 53, 67
Scorpion Fish, 53, **61**, 67, 69, **79**, 80, 127
Seahorse, 19, **20**, 50, **51**, 58, 70, **85**, 98,106, **140**, **141**
Sea Temperature, 11
Sennet, 17, 51, 75
Sergeant Major Fish, 13, 33, **58**, 57, 97, 105
  Eggs, **57**
Sharks, 19
  Nurse, **46**, **47**, 121
Shrimp,
  Banded Coral, 51, 59, 75, **83**, 98, 117
  Cleaner, 27, 59, 98, 101, 111,
  Peppermint, **21**
  Red Snapping, **21**
  Mantis Shrimp, 75, **98**, 99
  Ciliated, **21**
  Giant Mantis **105**
Snapper, 13, 17, 33, 35, 127
  Glasseye Snapper, 69, 75, 101
Snorkelling, 13, 23, 97
Spawning,
Sponge, 19, 22, **51**,
  Barrel, 22, 49, 51, 55, **67**, 75, 103, 106, **107**, 117, **128**
  Branching Antler, **48**, **60**
  Brown Octopus, 22, 123, 125
  Green Finger, 55, 63, 70, 81
  Lavender, **22**, 63, **122**
  Purple Finger, 49, **54**, 55, 75, **85**
  Red Encrusting, **23**, **78**, 122
  Orange Elephant Ear, 49, 54, 55, 63, 70, 109, **128**
  Yellow Tube, 16, **23**, 49, 55, **63**, 65, 70, 75, 83, **90**, 95, **108**, **116**
Spotted Drum, 53, 63, 75,

Squirrelfish, 13, **28**, 49, 55, **60**, 69, 79, 85, 97, 101, 121
Starfish, 13, 33, 35
S.S Stavronikita, The Wreck **23**, 23, 86-90
Sugar Cane, 11
Surgeon Fish, 13

T. Tarpon, 16, 17, 53, 67
Triggerfish, Grey, 53
Trumpetfish, 13, 35, 57, 61, 69, 75, **103**, 115, 129
Trunkfish, 13, 63, 83, 129
Tube Worm, 59, 79
Turtle, 15, 17, 18-**19**, 22, 49, 53, 55, 67, 69, 71, 89
  Eggs, **18**
  Green, 13, 18, **114**, 115
  Hawksbill, **13**, 18, **22**, 31, **62**, 79, **95**, 105, 115, 127
  Leatherback, 18, 29, 131

U. Urchin, Sea 13, **79**
Magnificent, **42**-**43**, **53**
Red Heart, 58
UV - Ultra Violet Light diving, **37**

W. West Side Scuba, 40-41
Whaleshark, 16, 18
Whales, Humpback, 18
Whips, Sea 16, 75, **84**, 109, 113, 127
  Red Sea **64**, 65
Wrasse,
  Bluehead Cleaner, 13, **65**, 99, 125
  Creole, 17, 23, 49, **63**, 65, 77, **80**, 81, **87**
Wrecks, 13, 15, **23**, **56**, 57, 89, **106**, 135

Y. Yellow Goatfish, 17, 57, 65, 81, 98, 127
Yellow Submarine, **59**